CONTENTS（目次）

LESSON 1	現在と過去を表す表現	4
LESSON 2	未来を表す表現	10
LESSON 3	助動詞	16
LESSON 4	完了形	22
LESSON 5	受動態	28
LESSON 6	比較①（比較級，最上級）	34
LESSON 7	比較②（同等比較，倍数比較など）	40
LESSON 8	動名詞	46
LESSON 9	to 不定詞	52
LESSON 10	分詞	58
LESSON 11	関係詞①（関係代名詞）	64
LESSON 12	関係詞②（関係副詞）	70
LESSON 13	仮定法	76
LESSON 14	特殊構文	82
2年の総合問題 第1回		88
第2回		90
第3回		92
不規則動詞変化表		94
形容詞・副詞比較変化表		96

本書の構成と使い方

このワークブックは，APPLAUSE ENGLISH LOGIC AND EXPRESSION II の内容にしたがって作られています。教科書各課の Focus に出てくる文法事項の練習問題を，STEP 1 から 3 にかけて段階的に解いていく構成となっています。予習だけでなく，復習やテスト前の整理にも活用できます。各ページの内容は次のとおりです。

STEP 1 基本問題

文法項目ごとに，整序問題や英文和訳問題などを用意しています。
まずはこのステップで，それぞれの文法項目の基礎を確認しましょう。

STEP 2 実践問題

STEP 1 より少し難易度が上がった問題を用意しています。
さまざまな形式の問題を解いて，着実に文法項目を身につけましょう。

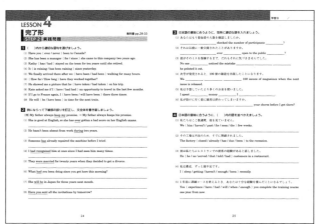

右のQRコードをタブレット端末で読み取ると、音声のウェブページにつながります。次のURLからもアクセスできます。
https://www.kairyudo.co.jp/applause2lewb

STEP 3 まとめ問題

和文英訳問題など、英語でのライティングを練習できる問題が配置されています。これまでに身につけた文法事項を用いてどこまで発信できるか確認しましょう。
また、教科書の各課 Model Dialog の音声を用いたディクテーション問題も用意しました。

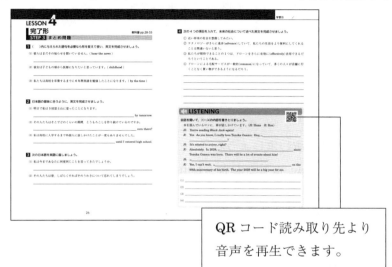

QRコード読み取り先より音声を再生できます。

■ 2年の総合問題

1年間で学んだ文法事項を総復習するページです。3回に分かれた総合問題を解くことで、年間をとおして学んだ内容の定着度を確認できます。

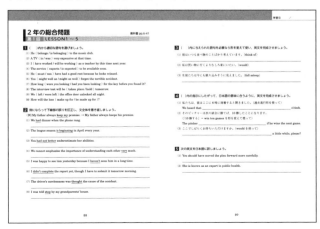

LESSON 1

現在と過去を表す表現

教科書 pp.6-11

STEP 1 基本問題

① 現在形

1 日本語の意味に合うように（　　）内の語を並べかえ，文全体を書き直しましょう。

(1) 彼は私が困っているといつも助けてくれます。

He (I'm / me / whenever / helps) in trouble.

_____

(2) 私の子どもはいつもリビングで眠ってしまいます。

My child (falls / always / asleep) in the living room.

_____

(3) 列車でそこに到着するのにどれくらいの時間がかかりますか。

How long (does / take / it / to) get there by train?

_____

2 次の英文を日本語に訳しましょう。

He's usually at home on the days when he doesn't work.

_____

② 過去形

1 日本語の意味に合うように（　　）内の語を並べかえ，文全体を書き直しましょう。

(1) ジャガイモは西暦 1600 年頃に日本にやって来ました。

Potatoes (Japan / around / to / came) 1600.

_____

(2) 後ろから声が聞こえました。だれか私を呼びましたか。

I heard a voice behind me. (me / call / did / anyone)?

_____

(3) 彼はなぜ今朝仕事に遅れたの？

(was / late / he / why) for work this morning?

_____

2 次の英文を日本語に訳しましょう。

The hall was full of people when we went to a concert there.

_____

❸ 現在進行形

1　日本語の意味に合うように（　　）内の語を並べかえ，文全体を書き直しましょう。

(1) 私はあなたが来るのを楽しみにしています。

I (forward / am / to / looking) your visit.

_____

(2) その製品はまだ売れ続けています。

The product (is / well / selling / still).

_____

(3) どんな種類の仕事を探しているのですか。

What kind of job (looking / are / for / you)?

_____

2　次の英文を日本語に訳しましょう。

How are you preparing for the difficult exam?

_____

❹ 過去進行形

1　日本語の意味に合うように（　　）内の語を並べかえ，文全体を書き直しましょう。

(1) 雨がひどく降っていたのに，出かけたのですか。

Did you go out even though (was / raining / it) heavily?

_____

(2) 眼鏡をかけていたので，あなただと気づきませんでした。

I didn't realize it was you because (were / you / wearing) glasses.

_____

(3) 図書館でだれと勉強していたのですか。

Who (you / were / with / studying) in the library?

_____

2　次の英文を日本語に訳しましょう。

I was just telling Misa about the event we are going to attend together.

_____

LESSON 1
現在と過去を表す表現

教科書 pp.6-11

STEP 2 実践問題

1 ( )内から適切な語句を選びましょう。

(1) We (practice / are practicing) baseball only on weekends.

(2) I (see / saw) Ms. Tanaka a minute ago at the entrance.

(3) We (go / are going) to a movie together now and then.

(4) You (resemble / are resembling) the famous actor in appearance.

(5) (Are you belonging / Do you belong) to the music club at school?

(6) He (gets / got) home from shopping just now.

(7) Most students know that the sun (rose / rises) in the east.

(8) Please be quiet because we (are having / have) an important discussion now.

(9) Our city library (is having / has) tens of thousands of books and magazines.

(10) Someone (uses / was using) the computer when I was here.

2 例にならって下線部の誤りを訂正し，文全体を書き直しましょう。

（例）My father always keep my promise. → My father always keeps his promise.

(1) I was taking the picture when I visited Hokkaido.

_____

(2) Is Helen having a job now?

_____

(3) Do you know when World War II ends?

_____

(4) I talked with Sam on the phone when Mary came in.

_____

(5) How do you get to the downtown area before?

_____

(6) Can you see the man who walks toward us?

_____

(7) We are knowing that he made a mistake.

_____

(8) What did you do when I called you last night?

_____

3 日本語の意味に合うように，空所に適切な語を入れましょう。

(1) 彼は今日はずいぶん静かですね。

He ＿＿＿＿＿＿ ＿＿＿＿＿＿ very quiet today.

(2) 痛みが徐々に消えつつあり，安心しています。

I am relieved that the ＿＿＿＿＿＿ ＿＿＿＿＿＿ ＿＿＿＿＿＿ gradually.

(3) 私の家は東京にありますが，今は福岡に滞在しています。

Although my house is in Tokyo, I ＿＿＿＿＿＿ ＿＿＿＿＿＿ in Fukuoka now.

(4) テレビを見ていないなら，消してください。

Turn off the TV if you ＿＿＿＿＿＿ ＿＿＿＿＿＿ it.

(5) 彼女はちょうど会社を出たところです。

She ＿＿＿＿＿＿ ＿＿＿＿＿＿ the office.

(6) 彼らは注意深く，私の話に耳を傾けていました。

They ＿＿＿＿＿＿ ＿＿＿＿＿＿ ＿＿＿＿＿＿ me carefully.

4 日本語の意味に合うように，（　　）内の語句を並べかえましょう。

(1) 金曜日に授業はいくつあるの？

(you / many / do / how / classes / have) on Fridays?

＿＿＿＿＿＿＿＿＿＿＿＿＿＿＿＿＿＿＿＿＿＿＿＿＿＿＿＿＿＿＿＿

(2) 彼がスピーチをしている間に眠くなりました。

I became sleepy (while / a speech / was / making / he).

＿＿＿＿＿＿＿＿＿＿＿＿＿＿＿＿＿＿＿＿＿＿＿＿＿＿＿＿＿＿＿＿

(3) 昨晩，宿題を終わらせるために遅くまで起きていました。

I (last / up / to / late / night / stayed) finish my homework.

＿＿＿＿＿＿＿＿＿＿＿＿＿＿＿＿＿＿＿＿＿＿＿＿＿＿＿＿＿＿＿＿

(4) 彼女はいつもひとの悪口ばかり言っています。

She (bad / something / is / saying / about / always) others.

＿＿＿＿＿＿＿＿＿＿＿＿＿＿＿＿＿＿＿＿＿＿＿＿＿＿＿＿＿＿＿＿

(5) 私の母は最近になるまで車の運転をやめませんでした。

My mother (driving / didn't / a car / give up / recently / until).

＿＿＿＿＿＿＿＿＿＿＿＿＿＿＿＿＿＿＿＿＿＿＿＿＿＿＿＿＿＿＿＿

(6) 事故があったとき，あなたは何をしようとしていたのですか。

(were / what / to / do / you / trying) when the accident happened?

＿＿＿＿＿＿＿＿＿＿＿＿＿＿＿＿＿＿＿＿＿＿＿＿＿＿＿＿＿＿＿＿

LESSON 1
現在と過去を表す表現
教科書 pp.6-11
STEP 3 まとめ問題

1 ( )内に与えられた語句を必要なら形を変えて使い，英文を完成させましょう。

(1) 私は子どもの頃，祖母とよく散歩をしました。(take a walk / when)

_____

(2) 私たちは彼女のためにパーティーを開く計画をしているところです。(plan / have)

_____

(3) 昨年の今頃，私は猛勉強していました。(study hard / about this time last year)

_____

2 日本語の意味に合うように，英文を完成させましょう。

(1) 私はいったんピアノを弾き始めると，ピアノを弾くことに熱中します。

_____ once I begin playing it.

(2) 生徒たちがそこへいすを移動させているので，今その部屋は使えません。

You cannot use the room right now _____.

(3) 家の近くをジョギングしていたとき，その看板に気づきました。

I noticed the sign _____ in my neighborhood.

3 次の日本語を英語に直しましょう。

(1) 紙の本を買わない日本人が増えています。

_____

(2) あなたは昨日，駅でだれかを待っていたのですか。

_____

4 次の4つの項目を入れて,「私」が昨年1年間頑張ったことや今後の目標について英語で発表しましょう。

① すべての教科の中で理科をいちばん頑張って勉強した。理科は好きだし,将来科学者となって環境を保護する(protect the environment)と決めたからである。
② 学校でクラブには所属していなかったが,学校や地域(in my community)でボランティア活動に積極的に参加した(actively take part in)。
③ 趣味は魚釣りで,ときどき川に魚釣りに出かける。今年は渓流釣り(fishing in a mountain stream)に挑戦してみたい。
④ 今年は芸術や音楽などの苦手な科目にも頑張って取り組みたい。

_____
_____
_____
_____

🔊 LISTENING

会話を聞いて,(1)~(4)の内容を書きとりましょう。
　拓は,エイミーと部活動について話しています。(*A*: Amy　*T*: Taku)

A: (1)_____.
T: Yeah! It's because I have some important games soon. By the way, (2)_____?
A: Well, (3)_____. In fact, club activities in Australia are different from those in Japan.
T: Is it? Tell me more.
A: In some parts of Australia, club activities themselves are one of the subjects like math or science. Furthermore, we don't have any club activities after school or on weekends.
T: Really? (4)_____.

(1) _____
(2) _____
(3) _____
(4) _____

LESSON 2

未来を表す表現

教科書 pp.12-17

STEP 1 基本問題

❶ 現在形

1 日本語の意味に合うように（　　）内の語句を並べかえ，文全体を書き直しましょう。

(1) 明日の朝，私は東京に向けて出発します。

I (for / Tokyo / leave) tomorrow morning.

_____

(2) 今年の夏休みはいつ始まるのですか。

(the summer vacation / start / does / when) this year?

_____

(3) このバスは 7 時に目的地に着きます。

This bus (at / arrives / its destination) at seven.

_____

2 次の英文を日本語に訳しましょう。

The show runs through the end of this month.

_____

❷ 現在進行形・過去進行形

1 日本語の意味に合うように（　　）内の語句を並べかえ，文全体を書き直しましょう。

(1) 彼らは来月，結婚します。

(are / married / getting / they) next month.

_____

(2) その時間は会議に出席しているので，4 時に会うことはできません。

We can't meet at four (I'm / because / a meeting / attending) at that time.

_____

(3) 私はリサ(Lisa)がパーティーでスピーチをすると思っていました。

I thought (was / a speech / giving / Lisa) at the party.

_____

2 次の英文を日本語に訳しましょう。

I thought he was coming to my house at four.

_____

10

❸ 未来進行形

1 日本語の意味に合うように（　　）内の語を並べかえ，文全体を書き直しましょう。

(1) 彼らは 7 時頃には夕食を食べているよ。

(will / having / be / dinner / they) around seven.

_____

(2) 明日はだれかオフィスで作業していますか。

(anyone / be / working / will) in the office tomorrow?

_____

2 次の英文を日本語に訳しましょう。

The weather forecast says it will be snowing when we get to Hokkaido.

_____

❹ 未来を表すその他の表現

1 日本語の意味に合うように（　　）内の語を並べかえ，文全体を書き直しましょう。

(1) 私はちょうどピザを頼むところでした。

I (order / just / to / was / about) some pizza.

_____

(2) 私たちはそこに長く滞在する予定ではありません。

We (to / stay / aren't / planning) there for a long time.

_____

2 次の英文を日本語に訳しましょう。

The building is expected to take two years to complete.

_____

LESSON 2
未来を表す表現
STEP 2 実践問題

教科書 pp.12-17

1 ( )内から適切な語句を選びましょう。

(1) I (want / am wanting) to go to the beach soon after I arrive in Hawaii.

(2) Who (do you think / are you thinking) will be the winner?

(3) They (are starting / were starting) to prepare when I returned.

(4) My cousin (gets / is getting) married next month.

(5) I heard that her birthday (came / was coming) soon.

(6) She (will fly / will be flying) to New York by this time tomorrow.

(7) I (stay / am going to stay) home all day tomorrow.

(8) I (am thinking of / was thinking of) going surfing, but I changed my mind.

(9) You (work for / will be working for) the same company in a year.

(10) We (are planning / were planning) to build our house in 2021, but we haven't started yet.

2 例にならって下線部の誤りを訂正し，文全体を書き直しましょう。

(例) My father always keep my promise. → My father always keeps his promise.

(1) Two trains to Tokyo left in the next hour.

_____

(2) He was coming here again sometime in the near future.

_____

(3) I am promising you that I won't tell a lie.

_____

(4) The flower shop was opening in thirty minutes.

_____

(5) Many people will watch the game on TV when you go to the theater.

_____

(6) We are about to practice soccer outside when it started raining.

_____

(7) Will he still run in the park tomorrow morning?

_____

(8) The movie expects to be a big hit.

_____

3 日本語の意味に合うように，空所に適切な語を入れましょう。

(1) 私たちのグループは 2 ～ 3 日したらそのプロジェクトに取り組み始めます。

Our group ＿＿＿＿＿＿ ＿＿＿＿＿＿ working on the project ＿＿＿＿＿＿ a few days.

(2) メアリーは今日，あなたのパーティーに来るの？

Is Mary ＿＿＿＿＿＿ ＿＿＿＿＿＿ your party today?

(3) 彼は本当のことを言うつもりでした。

He ＿＿＿＿＿＿ ＿＿＿＿＿＿ ＿＿＿＿＿＿ ＿＿＿＿＿＿ the truth.

(4) あなたがそこに着いたとき，みんながあなたを待っているでしょう。

They all ＿＿＿＿＿＿ ＿＿＿＿＿＿ ＿＿＿＿＿＿ for you when you get there.

(5) 私たちは故郷に戻ろうと計画しています。

We ＿＿＿＿＿＿ ＿＿＿＿＿＿ ＿＿＿＿＿＿ return to our hometown.

(6) 私は午後 3 時までにその報告書を終わらせないといけません。

I ＿＿＿＿＿＿ ＿＿＿＿＿＿ ＿＿＿＿＿＿ the report by 3 p.m.

4 日本語の意味に合うように，（　　）内の語句を並べかえましょう。

(1) 午前 11 時に名古屋駅に到着する列車に乗ってください。

(that / at / take / arrives / the train) Nagoya Station at 11 a.m.

_____

(2) あなたが部屋を掃除している間，彼らがそこでいすを移動させているでしょう。

While you are cleaning the room, they (chairs / be / will / there / moving).

_____

(3) 私は多くの生徒が今日，工場に来るものと聞いていました。

I heard that (coming / many students / were / our factory / to) today.

_____

(4) 明後日，デートなのです。

I (day / have / tomorrow / after / a date / the).

_____

(5) 私は今日の午前に医者に診てもらいに行きます。

I will (a doctor / morning / to / this / go / see).

_____

(6) さっきは何を言いかけたの？

(about / you / to / say / what / were) a few minutes ago?

_____

LESSON 2
未来を表す表現

教科書 pp.12-17

STEP 3 まとめ問題

1 (   )内の指示にしたがって，与えられた語句を必要なら形を変えて使い，英文を完成させましょう。

(1) 今年は4月に野球シーズンが始まります。（現在形を使って）

_____ this year.

(2) 私は今の仕事が好きなので，10年後もそこで働いているでしょう。

（未来進行形を使って）

I like my current job, so _____ in 10 years.

(3) サチが日曜日にここに来ると聞いていました。（過去進行形を使って）

I heard that Sachi _____.

(4) 荷物がいつ到着するのかを問い合わせるために電話しています。（現在進行形を使って）

I'm calling to ask _____.

(5) 外はすぐに暗くなるよ。（現在進行形を使って，get dark）

_____ soon.

(6) 私たちはAチームと対戦することになっています。

（suppose を形を変えて使って，play against）

We _____ team A.

2 次の日本語を英語に直しましょう。

(1) パーティーには100人が参加すると予想されます。

_____

(2) 私はちょうど自分のアイデアを説明しようとしていたところでした。

_____

3 次の4つの項目を入れて，タケシの自己紹介を英語で表してみましょう。

① 小さい頃，動物の飼育員（a zookeeper）になりたかった。動物園でいろいろな種類の動物を見るのが好きだったからである。

② 今はコンピュータを使った仕事に興味がある。授業で自分が作ったホームページに満足したからである。

③ 将来はwebデザイナーになって，多くの人や企業が情報を発信する役に立ちたい。

④ 自分の夢を実現するために，専門コース（specialized courses）のある学校に進み，資格を取得（get qualifications）したい。

_____

_____

_____

_____

_____

🔊 LISTENING

会話を聞いて，(1)〜(4)の内容を書きとりましょう。
学校からの帰り道に，ロンとエイミーが話しています。（*R:* Ron　*A:* Amy）

R: (1)_____?

A: (2)_____. Why?

R: According to the weather forecast, we may be able to see a meteor shower then.

A: What is a "meteor shower"?

R: It means a lot of shooting stars can be seen at the same time.

A: Fantastic! If I see many shooting stars, (3)_____.

R: How exciting! (4)_____.

A: I hope the sky will be clear.

(1) _____

(2) _____

(3) _____

(4) _____

LESSON 3
助動詞

教科書 pp.20-25

STEP 1 基本問題

❶ 依頼

1 日本語の意味に合うように（　）内の語句を並べかえ，文全体を書き直しましょう。

(1) このバッグを部屋に運んでもらえますか。
   (this bag / you / can / carry) to the room?

   _____

(2) 食事の準備を手伝ってもらえますか。
   (help / will / me / you / prepare) a meal?

   _____

(3) 住所を教えていただけますか。
   (you / tell / please / would) me your address?

   _____

2 次の英文を日本語に訳しましょう。
   Could you give me a ride to the station?

   _____

❷ 推量・予測

1 日本語の意味に合うように（　）内の語を並べかえ，文全体を書き直しましょう。

(1) 列車が遅れているので，彼は遅れるかもしれません。
   He (be / might / late) because the train has been delayed.

   _____

(2) 彼女はすでに家を出発しているので，そこに間に合うはずです。
   She has already left home, so she (there / should / get) on time.

   _____

2 次の英文を日本語に訳しましょう。
   He must have been surprised to see his teacher there.

   _____

❸ 助言・後悔

1　日本語の意味に合うように(　　)内の語を並べかえ，文全体を書き直しましょう。

(1) そのことをよく考えるべきです。

You (it / think / should / about) carefully.

_____

(2) お母さんが帰ってくる前に台所を片付けなくちゃ。

We (better / had / clean) the kitchen before Mom gets back.

_____

(3) 大きな台風が近づいているので，今夜は外出しないようにしなさい。

You (go / better / not / had) out tonight because a big typhoon is coming.

_____

2　次の英文を日本語に訳しましょう。

He should have been responsible for the loss.

_____

❹ 助動詞を用いたさまざまな表現

1　日本語の意味に合うように(　　)内の語を並べかえ，文全体を書き直しましょう。

(1) 私はむしろ家で夕食をとりたい。

I (rather / dinner / have / would) at home.

_____

(2) 人混みは避けた方がいいですよ。

You (might / well / as / avoid) the crowd.

_____

2　次の英文を日本語に訳しましょう。

You really saved me. I cannot thank you too much.

_____

LESSON 3

助動詞
教科書 pp.20-25

STEP 2 実践問題

1 ( )内から適切な語句を選びましょう。

(1) (Should / Can) you repair my bike by tomorrow?

(2) (Would / Might) you briefly introduce yourself, please?

(3) I can't find my smartphone. I (should have / must have) left it on the train.

(4) I (have might to / might have to) go to the office tomorrow.

(5) You (ought / should) consider every possibility.

(6) (Have / Will) you give us your opinion?

(7) I (should have not / should not have) bought such expensive clothes.

(8) (Shall / Could) you place an order online?

(9) You (might not as well / might as well not) keep any pets if you can't take good care of them.

(10) You (can be never / can never be) too cautious when driving a car.

2 例にならって下線部の誤りを訂正し，文全体を書き直しましょう。

(例) My father always <u>keep my</u> promise. → My father always keeps his promise.

(1) Will <u>show you</u> me the way to the station?

_____

(2) He looks very tired. He <u>should</u> have worked too hard.

_____

(3) The story <u>would</u> be true, but none of us believe it.

_____

(4) You <u>had not better</u> give your children snacks before meals.

_____

(5) Both of them <u>cannot</u> share the information because they will attend the meeting.

_____

(6) I asked you to buy ten ice cream cones, but <u>please you could</u> get one more?

_____

(7) I <u>would not rather</u> drink the spicy juice.

_____

(8) He doesn't have enough money to study abroad. He <u>must</u> have saved more money.

_____

3 日本語の意味に合うように，空所に適切な語を入れましょう。

(1) 今日，少し残業してくれますか。

＿＿＿＿＿＿ ＿＿＿＿＿＿ ＿＿＿＿＿＿ overtime a bit today?

(2) 答えを見つけるのは難しくないはずです。

It ＿＿＿＿＿＿ ＿＿＿＿＿＿ ＿＿＿＿＿＿ to find an answer.

(3) あなたが戻ってくるのを待つべきですか。

＿＿＿＿＿＿ I ＿＿＿＿＿＿ ＿＿＿＿＿＿ you to come back?

(4) 計画に賛成であれば，挙手していただけますでしょうか。

＿＿＿＿＿＿ ＿＿＿＿＿＿ ＿＿＿＿＿＿ your hand if you agree with the plan?

(5) 私はそこへ車で行くよりもむしろ歩いて行きたい。

I ＿＿＿＿＿＿ ＿＿＿＿＿＿ go there on foot ＿＿＿＿＿＿ by car.

(6) 車で空港まで迎えに行きましょうか。

＿＿＿＿＿＿ ＿＿＿＿＿＿ pick you up at the airport?

4 日本語の意味に合うように，（　　）内の語句を並べかえましょう。

(1) 大事なことは，あらかじめ教えてもらえますか。

(me / can / important / tell / something / you) beforehand?

＿＿＿＿＿＿＿＿＿＿＿＿＿＿＿＿＿＿＿＿＿＿＿＿＿＿＿＿＿＿

(2) いっしょに書類を探してもらえますか。

(you / for / look / the document / will) with me?

＿＿＿＿＿＿＿＿＿＿＿＿＿＿＿＿＿＿＿＿＿＿＿＿＿＿＿＿＿＿

(3) あなたは私たちを待たせたことを詫びるべきです。

You (for / wait / making / us / should / apologize).

＿＿＿＿＿＿＿＿＿＿＿＿＿＿＿＿＿＿＿＿＿＿＿＿＿＿＿＿＿＿

(4) その予定表を E メールで送っていただけますでしょうか。

(could / me / e-mail / send / you / by / the schedule), please?

＿＿＿＿＿＿＿＿＿＿＿＿＿＿＿＿＿＿＿＿＿＿＿＿＿＿＿＿＿＿

(5) 海外ではチップを渡すのを忘れないようにした方がいいです。

You (remember / give / had / tips / to / better) overseas.

＿＿＿＿＿＿＿＿＿＿＿＿＿＿＿＿＿＿＿＿＿＿＿＿＿＿＿＿＿＿

(6) テスト勉強をもっとしておけばよかった。

I (have / should / more / for / studied) the test.

＿＿＿＿＿＿＿＿＿＿＿＿＿＿＿＿＿＿＿＿＿＿＿＿＿＿＿＿＿＿

LESSON 3
助動詞

教科書 pp.20-25

STEP 3 まとめ問題

1 ( )内に与えられた語句を必要なら形を変えて使い，英文を完成させましょう。

(1) テーブルの上の塩を取っていただけませんか。(pass)

_____

(2) 私たちは彼女をどんなにほめてもほめ足りないです。(praise)

_____

(3) 彼は道を間違えたに違いありません。(take the wrong road)

_____

2 日本語の意味に合うように，英文を完成させましょう。

(1) 私たちは急いだら，列車に間に合うかもしれません。

_____ if we hurry.

(2) ここはすべりやすいので，足元に気をつけた方がいいです。

You _____ because it's slippery here.

(3) 何度も見直したので，ミスはないはずです。

_____ because we checked it many times.

3 次の日本語を英語に直しましょう。

(1) ここでの喫煙は控えていただけますか。

_____

(2) あなたはもっと早く警察を呼ぶべきでした。

_____

4 次の3つの項目を入れて，SNSの使い方に関する英文を作ってみましょう。

① SNSを正しく使うためには，私たちそれぞれがその利点と不利な点を把握すべきである。

② 私がSNSのいちばんの利点と思うことの1つは，災害時(in times of disaster)に非常に有効であることである。SNSを通じてより簡単に重要な情報を発信・収集することができるからである。

③ 一方で，私たちが注意すべきことは，SNSで自由に意見を述べると，他者を傷つける可能性があることである。自分の発言(remarks)が人にどのように影響(affect)し得るかを常に考える必要がある。

_____
_____
_____
_____

🔊 LISTENING

会話を聞いて，(1)〜(4)の内容を書きとりましょう。

エイミーは拓に腹を立てているようです。(*A*: Amy *T*: Taku)

A: I know you usually post pictures on the web. However, when I saw your post yesterday, I got angry.

T: Did you? (1)_____.

A: You posted my picture without my permission. (2)_____
_____.

T: I'm terribly sorry. (3)_____.

A: It's OK. I was just surprised.

T: Posting pictures on social media might have both advantages and disadvantages. Therefore, (4)_____.

(1) _____
(2) _____
(3) _____
(4) _____

LESSON 4

完了形

教科書 pp.28-33

STEP 1 基本問題

❶ 現在完了形

1　日本語の意味に合うように（　　）内の語を並べかえ，文全体を書き直しましょう。

(1) 私はすでに空港に到着しています。
　　I (already / have / arrived) at the airport.

(2) ジェーンは一度，京都に行ったことがあります。
　　Jane (visited / once / Kyoto / has).

(3) 私たちは今朝から忙しいです。
　　We (have / busy / since / been) this morning.

2　次の英文を日本語に訳しましょう。
　　I have just been to the city library to borrow a book.

❷ 過去完了形

1　日本語の意味に合うように（　　）内の語を並べかえ，文全体を書き直しましょう。

(1) 私がスタジアムに着いたときには，試合はすでに終わっていました。
　　When I got to the stadium, the game (finished / had / already).

(2) それまで私は飛行機に乗ったことがありませんでした。
　　I (had / been / on / never) a plane before that.

(3) 彼は3日間何も食べていないと言いました。
　　He said (not / eaten / had / he) for three days.

2　次の英文を日本語に訳しましょう。
　　The shop gave me my money back before I requested a refund.

❸ 現在完了進行形・過去完了進行形

1　日本語の意味に合うように（　　）内の語句を並べかえ，文全体を書き直しましょう。

(1) その人たちは工事現場で一日中大きな騒音を出し続けています。

They (making / have / been / a lot of) noise at the construction site all day.

_____

(2) 彼は2年前まで自分の事業を運営し続けていました。

He (running / had / been) his own business until two years ago.

_____

2　次の英文を日本語に訳しましょう。

We have been waiting for the customer for an hour, but he hasn't arrived.

_____

❹ 未来完了形

1　日本語の意味に合うように（　　）内の語を並べかえ，文全体を書き直しましょう。

(1) 試験は次の水曜日までに終わってしまうでしょう。

The exams (finished / have / will) by next Wednesday.

_____

(2) もうすぐ彼と知り合って10年になります。

I (will / him / known / have) for ten years before long.

_____

2　次の英文を日本語に訳しましょう。

The museum will have received one thousand visitors when the next one walks through the door.

_____

LESSON 4 完了形

教科書 pp.28-33

STEP 2 実践問題

1 (　)内から適切な語句を選びましょう。

(1) Have you (ever / never) been to Canada?
(2) She has been a manager (for / since) she came to this company two years ago.
(3) Kathy (has / had) stayed on the team for ten years until she retired.
(4) It (is raining / has been raining) since yesterday.
(5) We finally arrived there after we (have been / had been) walking for many hours.
(6) (How far / How long) have they worked together?
(7) He showed me a picture that he (have taken / had taken) on his trip.
(8) Kate asked me if I (have / had had) an opportunity to travel in the last few months.
(9) If I go to France again, I (have been / will have been) there three times.
(10) He will (be / have been) in time for the next train.

2 例にならって下線部の誤りを訂正し，文全体を書き直しましょう。

（例）My father always <u>keep my</u> promise. → My father always keeps his promise.

(1) She is good at English, so she has <u>ever</u> gotten a bad score on her English exams.
_____

(2) He hasn't been absent from work <u>during</u> two years.
_____

(3) Someone <u>has</u> already repaired the machine before I tried.
_____

(4) I <u>had recognized</u> him at once since I had seen him many times.
_____

(5) They <u>were married</u> for twenty years when they decided to get a divorce.
_____

(6) What <u>had</u> you been doing since you got here this morning?
_____

(7) She <u>will be</u> in Japan for three years next month.
_____

(8) <u>Have you sent</u> all the invitations by tomorrow?
_____

3 日本語の意味に合うように，空所に適切な語を入れましょう。

(1) あなたはもう参加者の人数を確認しましたか。

_____ _____ checked the number of participants _____?

(2) それは以前に一般公開されたことがありますか。

_____ _____ ever _____ open to the public _____?

(3) 彼がそのミスを指摘するまで，だれもそれに気づきませんでした。

No one _____ noticed the mistake _____ _____ _____

he pointed it out.

(4) 次号が発売されると，100 冊の雑誌を出版したことになります。

We _____ _____ _____ 100 issues of magazines when the next

issue is released.

(5) 私は予想していたより多くのお金を使いました。

I spent _____ money _____ I _____ _____.

(6) 私が助けに行く前に雑用は終わってしまいますか。

_____ _____ _____ _____ your chores before I get there?

4 日本語の意味に合うように，（　　）内の語を並べかえましょう。

(1) 私たちはここ数週間，彼を見ていません。

We (him / haven't / past / for / seen / the) few weeks.

_____

(2) その工場は不況のため，すでに閉鎖されました。

The factory (closed / already / has / due / been) to the recession.

_____

(3) 彼は私たちにレストランでの接客の経験があると話しました。

He (he / us / served / that / told / had) customers in a restaurant.

_____

(4) 私は最近，ずっと寝不足です。

I (sleep / getting / haven't / enough / been) recently.

_____

(5) 1 年後に訓練コースを終えるとき，あなたは十分な経験を積んだことになるでしょう。

You (experience / have / had / will / when / enough) you complete the training course

one year from now.

_____

LESSON 4
完了形
教科書 pp.28-33
STEP 3 まとめ問題

1 ( )内に与えられた語句を必要なら形を変えて使い，英文を完成させましょう。

(1) 彼らはまだその知らせを聞いていません。(hear the news)

_____

(2) 彼女は子どもの頃から医師になりたいと思っています。(childhood)

_____

(3) 私たちは高校を卒業するまでに 6 年間英語を勉強したことになります。(by the time)

_____

2 日本語の意味に合うように，英文を完成させましょう。

(1) 明日で私は 3 回富士山に登ったことになります。

_____ by tomorrow.

(2) その人たちはそこでどのくらいの期間，とうもろこしを作り続けているのですか。

_____ corn there?

(3) 私は高校に入学するまで外国人に話しかけたことが一度もありませんでした。

_____ until I entered high school.

3 次の日本語を英語に直しましょう。

(1) 私は今まであなたに何度同じことを言ってきたでしょうか。

_____

(2) その人たちは皆，しばらくすればそのうわさについて忘れてしまうでしょう。

_____

学習日　　／

4 次の4つの項目を入れて，未来の社会について述べた英文を完成させましょう。

① 近い将来の社会を想像してみたい。

② テクノロジーがさらに進歩(advance)していて，私たちの生活をより便利にしてくれることは間違いないと思う。

③ 私たちが期待できることの1つは，ドローンをさらに有効に(effectively)活用できるだろうということである。

④ ドローンによる宅配サービスが一般的(common)になっていて，多くの人々が店舗に行くことなく買い物ができるようになるだろう。

_____

_____

_____

_____

_____

🔊 LISTENING

会話を聞いて，(1)〜(4)の内容を書きとりましょう。

　本を読んでいるロンに，華が話しかけています。(*H*: Hana　*R*: Ron)

H:　You're reading *Black Jack* again!

R:　Yes. As you know, I really love Tezuka Osamu. Hey, (1)_____

_____?

H:　It's related to *anime*, right?

R:　Absolutely. In 2028, (2)_____ since

Tezuka Osamu was born. There will be a lot of events about him!

H:　(3)_____.

R:　Yes, I can't wait. (4)_____ on the

90th anniversary of his birth. The year 2028 will be a big year for me.

(1) _____

(2) _____

(3) _____

(4) _____

27

LESSON 5

受動態

教科書 pp.36-41

STEP 1 基本問題

❶ 基本的な受動態の用法

1 日本語の意味に合うように（　　　）内の語句を並べかえ，文全体を書き直しましょう。

(1) 京都は毎年，多くの人々によって訪れられます。

Kyoto (visited / is / by) many people every year.

_____

(2) この席はだれかが座っていますか。

(this seat / by / taken / is) anyone?

_____

(3) その本は明日までに図書館に返されなければなりません。

The book (be / returned / must) to the library by tomorrow.

_____

2 次の英文を日本語に訳しましょう。

The problem was dealt with by Tom.

_____

❷ 進行形・完了形の受動態

1 日本語の意味に合うように（　　　）内の語を並べかえ，文全体を書き直しましょう。

(1) その装置は多くの病院に導入されつつあります。

The device (being / is / introduced) into a lot of hospitals.

_____

(2) その事柄は長年，多くの科学者により観察されてきました。

The matter (been / by / has / observed) many scientists for years.

_____

2 次の英文を日本語に訳しましょう。

Have you been provided with everything you need?

_____

❸ SVOO, SVOC の受動態

1 日本語の意味に合うように（　　）内の語句を並べかえ，文全体を書き直しましょう。

(1) 私はその女性に駅までの道を尋ねられました。

I (the way / was / asked) to the station by the woman.

_____

(2) あなたの ID カードをスタッフの 1 人に見せる必要があります。

Your ID card (shown / to / must / be) one of the staff members.

_____

(3) タカシは略してタカと呼ばれているのですか。

(is / Taka / called / Takashi) for short?

_____

2 次の英文を日本語に訳しましょう。

They were left waiting outside for a long time.

_____

❹ 受動態を使ったさまざまな表現

1 日本語の意味に合うように（　　）内の語を並べかえ，文全体を書き直しましょう。

(1) 日本人は勤勉であるとよく言われます。

(it / often / is / said) that Japanese people are diligent.

_____

(2) その話が本当だと信じられていますか。

(is / that / believed / it) the story is true?

_____

2 次の英文を日本語に訳しましょう。

The country is incorrectly believed to be cold all year round.

_____

LESSON 5
受動態
教科書 pp.36-41

STEP 2 実践問題

1 次の文を受動態に書き直しましょう。

(1) She translated the sentences into English.

_____

(2) What language do the people of that country speak?

_____

(3) The police looked into the case.

_____

(4) We have to handle the problem carefully.

_____

(5) They reported that he was a competent engineer.

_____

2 例にならって下線部の誤りを訂正し，文全体を書き直しましょう。

（例）My father always keep my promise. → My father always keeps his promise.

(1) This article about the incident was found by the internet.

_____

(2) Vegetables tend to dislike by small children.

_____

(3) She is known by everyone in town.

_____

(4) Are the windows being cleaned every day?

_____

(5) He is thought that he is one of the best players in professional baseball.

_____

(6) A lot of homework is given for us by the teacher every day.

_____

(7) He was made be a doctor by his parents.

_____

(8) I was surprised at see English and Japanese written in her notebook.

_____

APPLAUSE
ENGLISH LOGIC AND EXPRESSION Ⅱ
ワークブック

解答・解説

開隆堂

LESSON 1
現在と過去を表す表現

(pp.4-9)

STEP 1　基本問題

❶ 1 (1) He helps me whenever I'm in
trouble.
(2) My child always falls asleep in the
living room.
(3) How long does it take to get there
by train?
2 彼はふだん，仕事のない日は家にいます。

解説
❶ 1 (1) whenever ～ は「～なときはいつも」
という意味。現在の習慣なので，現在
形で表す。

❷ 1 (1) Potatoes came to Japan around
1600.
(2) I heard a voice behind me．Did
anyone call me?
(3) Why was he late for work this
morning?
2 私たちがコンサートに行ったとき，そ
のホールは人でいっぱいでした。

解説
❷ 過去の出来事，状態や単発的な動作は過去
形で表す。

❸ 1 (1) I am looking forward to your visit.
(2) The product is still selling well.
(3) What kind of job are you looking
for?
2 あなたはどのようにしてその難しい試
験の準備をしているのですか。

解説
❸ 現在継続中であることは現在進行形で表す。
1 (1) look forward to ～「～を楽しみに待つ」

❹ 1 (1) Did you go out even though it was

raining heavily?
(2) I didn't realize it was you because
you were wearing glasses.
(3) Who were you studying with in the
library?
2 私はちょうどミサにいっしょに参加す
る予定のイベントについて話していた
ところでした。

解説
❹ 過去の一時点で継続中であったことは過去
進行形で表す。
1 (1) 出かけたときに雨が降っていたので，
過去進行形となる。

STEP 2　実践問題

1 (1) practice　　(2) saw　　(3) go
(4) resemble　　(5) Do you belong
(6) got　　(7) rises　　(8) are having
(9) has　　(10) was using

解説
1 (3) now and then は「時々」という意味。
ふだんの習慣を表す現在形を選ぶ。
(4) resemble ～「～に似ている」は状態を
表し，進行形にはならない。
(5) belong to ～「～に所属している」は状
態を表す動詞で，進行形にはならない。
(6) just now「たった今」は過去形とともに
使う。
(7)「太陽が東から昇る」などの不変の真理
は現在形で表す。
(8) have ～ は「～を持っている」以外の意
味(～を食べる，(会などを)開く など)で
は進行形にできる。

2 (1) I took the picture when I visited
Hokkaido.
(2) Does Helen have a job now?
(3) Do you know when World War II

ended?

(4) I was talking with Sam on the phone when Mary came in.

(5) How did you get to the downtown area before?

(6) Can you see the man who is walking toward us?

(7) We know that he made a mistake.

(8) What were you doing when I called you last night?

解説

2 (1)「写真を撮った」のは過去の単発的動作なので，過去形にする。

(2) have a job「仕事がある，職に就いている」は状態を表すので，進行形にはならない。

(3)「知っている」かどうかは現在のことだが，World War II が終わったのは過去のこと。

(4) when Mary came in「メアリーが入ってきたとき」は過去の一時点のことなので，過去進行形となる。

(6)「(今)私たちの方に向かって歩いている男性」なので，現在進行形にする。

(7) know ～「～を知っている」は状態を表す動詞で，進行形にはならない。

(8)「私が昨晩電話したとき」は過去の一時点のことなので，過去進行形となる。

3 (1) is being

(2) pain is disappearing

(3) am staying

(4) aren't watching

(5) just left

(6) were listening to

解説

3 (1)「(いつもはそうではないのに)今は～である」と言うときは be being の形を使う。

(3)「(今は)～に滞在している」と言う場合は現在進行形になる。

4 (1) How many classes do you have

(2) while he was making a speech

(3) stayed up late last night to

(4) is always saying something bad about

(5) didn't give up driving a car until recently

(6) What were you trying to do

解説

4 (4) be always ～ing は「いつも～ばかりしている[していた]」という意味になる。

(5)「最近になるまで車の運転をやめなかった」＝「最近になって車の運転をやめた」

STEP 3　まとめ問題

1 (1) I often took[used to take] a walk with my grandmother when I was a child.

(2) We are planning to have a party for her.

(3) I was studying hard about this time last year.

解説

1 (1)「よく散歩をした」のは過去の習慣なので，過去形にする。

(3) about this time last year「昨年の今頃」は一時点なので，進行形になる。

2 (1) I devote myself to playing the piano

(2) because students are moving chairs there

(3) when I was jogging

解説

2 (1) 現在の習慣を表すので，現在形にする。devote oneself to ～「～に熱中する」

3 (1) The number of Japanese who don't buy paper books is increasing. [There are more Japanese people

3

who don't purchase paper books.]
(2) Were you waiting for someone at the station yesterday?

country
(3) I practiced tennis in my school
(4) That's an interesting difference

解説
3 (1) number「数」を用い, the number of Japanese who ～「～する日本人の数」を主語にした文で表せる。the number of ～は単数であることに注意。「増えている」という変化の過程は現在進行形で表す。
(2) 「待っていた」は過去の一時点での継続中の動作なので, 過去進行形で表す。

4 (例) I'd like to talk about what I did last year. Last year, I studied science the hardest of all my subjects because I like science, so I decided to be a scientist and protect the environment in the future. I didn't belong to any clubs at school, but I actively took part in volunteer work at school and in my community. My hobby is fishing, and I sometimes go fishing in the river. I want to try fishing in a mountain stream this year. I'm going to work hard on my weak subjects such as art and music this year.

解説
4 ・decide to ～「～することに決める」
・take part in ～（= participate in ～）「～に参加する」
・be going to ～「～するつもりだ」

LISTENING

(1) You're practicing soccer very hard these days
(2) what club did you belong to in your

4

LESSON 2　(pp.10-15)
未来を表す表現

STEP 1　基本問題

❶ 1 (1) I leave for Tokyo tomorrow morning.
(2) When does the summer vacation start this year?
(3) This bus arrives at its destination at seven.
2 そのショーは今月末まで上演されます。

解説

❶ 現在形ですでに確定している予定を表すことができる。go, come, start, leave などの往来発着を表す動詞でよく使われる。
1 (1) leave for ～「～に向かって出発する」
2 run through ～「(物事が)～まで続く」

❷ 1 (1) They are getting married next month.
(2) We can't meet at four because I'm attending a meeting at that time.
(3) I thought Lisa was giving a speech at the party.
2 私は彼が4時に私の家に来ると思っていました。

解説

❷ 現在進行形は予定されている未来を，過去進行形は過去から見た未来を表すことができる。時間を表す語句とともに使うことが多い。
1 (3) 過去において予定されていたことを過去進行形で表す。

❸ 1 (1) They will be having dinner around seven.
(2) Will anyone be working in the office tomorrow?
2 天気予報によると, 私たちが北海道に到着する頃には雪が降っているでしょう。

解説

❸ 未来進行形は未来のある時点で進行中であると予想されることやする予定になっていることを表す。

❹ 1 (1) I was just about to order some pizza.
(2) We aren't planning to stay there for a long time.
2 その建物は完成するのに2年かかると予想されています。

解説

❹ 1 (1) be about to ～「まさに～しようとしている」
(2) be planning to ～「～することを予定している，～しようと思っている」
2 be expected to ～「～することが予想される，期待される」

STEP 2　実践問題

1 (1) want　(2) do you think
(3) were starting　(4) is getting
(5) was coming　(6) will be flying
(7) am going to stay
(8) was thinking of
(9) will be working for
(10) were planning

解説

1 (1) want to ～「～したい」は未来のことでも現在形で表す。
(4) 準備が整っている未来を現在進行形で表す。
(6) this time tomorrow「明日の今頃」未来の一時点で進行していることなので，未来進行形を選ぶ。
(7) be going to ～「～するつもりだ」
(8) be thinking of ～ ing「～しようと思っている」後が I changed my mind「気が変わった」と過去形になっているので，過

5

去進行形を選ぶ。

(9) in a year「今から1年後」未来の一時点で進行していることなので，未来進行形を選ぶ。

(10) we haven't started yet「家の建設をまだ始めていない」とあるので，were planning (to ～)「(～する) 予定であった」を選ぶ。

2 (1) Two trains to Tokyo leave [are leaving, will be leaving] in the next hour.
(2) He is [will be] coming here again sometime in the near future.
(3) I promise you that I won't tell a lie.
(4) The flower shop is [will be] opening in thirty minutes.
(5) Many people will be watching the game on TV when you go to the theater.
(6) We were about to practice soccer outside when it started raining.
(7) Will he still be running in the park tomorrow morning?
(8) The movie is expected to be a big hit.

解説
2 (3)「(未来のことを) 約束する」という場合でも現在形となる。
(5) 未来の一時点で進行していることなので，未来進行形を選ぶ。

3 (1) will start [begin], in
(2) coming to
(3) was going to tell
(4) will be waiting
(5) are planning to
(6) have to finish

解説
3 (5) be planning to ～「～しようと計画している，～しようと思っている」

(6) have to ～「～しなければならない」

4 (1) Take the train that arrives at
(2) will be moving chairs there
(3) many students were coming to our factory
(4) have a date the day after tomorrow
(5) go to see a doctor this morning
(6) What were you about to say

解説
4 (1) 往来発着などですでに確定している予定なので現在形で表すことができる。
(2)「あなたが掃除している間」は未来で進行していることなので，未来進行形にする。
(3) 過去進行形で過去から見た未来を表す。
(4) the day after tomorrow「明後日」
「一昨日」は the day before yesterday
(5) go to ＋動詞の原形～「～しに行く」
(6)「言いかけた」→「まさに言おうとした」

STEP 3 まとめ問題

1 (1) The baseball season starts in April
(2) I will be working there
(3) was coming here on Sunday
(4) when the [my] package is arriving
(5) It's getting dark outside
(6) are supposed to play against

解説
1 (1) すでに確定している予定を現在形で表す。
(2) 10年後に進行していることなので，未来進行形で表す。
(3) 過去進行形は過去から見た未来を表すことができる。
(5) get dark「暗くなる」
(6) be supposed to ～「～することになっている」

2 (1) One hundred people are expected to attend the party.
(2) I was (just) about to explain my idea.

next Monday
(3) I'll be able to make many wishes
(4) I am going to take a video

解説

2 (1) one hundred people「100人の人々」を主語にする。「～することが予想される」はbe expected to ～で表す。「～に参加する，～に出席する」の意味のattendは他動詞なので，前置詞は不要。
(2)「（ちょうど）～しようとする［した］ところだ」はbe (just) about to ～で表す。

3 (例) When I was little, I wanted to be a zookeeper because I liked seeing various kinds of animals at a zoo. I'm now interested in jobs using computers because I was satisfied with the homepage I made in a class. I hope that I'll be working as a web designer in the future and help a lot of people and companies send information online. To make my dream come true, I will go to a school that has specialized courses and get qualifications.

解説

3 ・「～することが好きだ」はlike ～ingまたはlike to ～で表す。
・be satisfied with ～「～に満足している」
・help O (to) ～「Oが～するのを手伝う，Oが～する役に立つ」
・make O ＋動詞の原形～「Oに～させる」
come true「実現する」

LISTENING

(1) What will you be doing tonight
(2) I'll be preparing for the final exam on

7

LESSON 3 (pp.16-21)
助動詞

STEP 1 基本問題

❶1(1)Can you carry this bag to the room?
　(2)Will you help me prepare a meal?
　(3)Would you please tell me your address?
　2駅まで乗せていっていただけますか。

解説
❶ Can［Will］you ～？は相手に何かをしてくれるように頼むときに用いる。Would［Could］を使うと丁寧な依頼になる。

❷1(1)He might be late because the train has been delayed.
　(2)She has already left home, so she should get there on time.
　2彼はそこで先生と会って驚いたに違いありません。

解説
❷1(1)might ～は可能性・推量「(ひょっとして)～かもしれない」を表すときによく用いられる。
　2must have ＋過去分詞～「～したに違いない」

❸1(1)You should think about it carefully.
　(2)We had better clean the kitchen before Mom gets back.
　(3)You had better not go out tonight because a big typhoon is coming.
　2彼がその損失の責任を負うべきだったのに。

解説
❸1(2)(3)had better ＋動詞の原形～で「～した方がいい(命令・義務のニュアンスに近い)」という意味。had better で 1 つの助動詞の役割があるため，not を入

れる場合は，better の後に置く。

❹1(1)I would rather have dinner at home.
　(2)You might as well avoid the crowd.
　2あなたのおかげで本当に助かりました。あなたには感謝してもしすぎることはありません。

解説
❹2cannot ＋動詞の原形～ too で「～してもしすぎることはない」を表す。

STEP 2 実践問題

1(1)Can　(2)Would　(3)must have
　(4)might have to　(5)should
　(6)Will　(7)should not have
　(8)Could　(9)might as well not
　(10)can never be

解説
1(5)「～すべきだ」という意味の should。ought を使う場合は ought to ＋動詞の原形となる。
　(7)should have ＋過去分詞～は「～すべきだったのに(しなかった)」を表す。not を入れる場合は位置に注意。
　(9)might as well ＋動詞の原形～は「～してはどうか，～した方がましだ」を表す。might as well で 1 つの助動詞の役割があるため，not を入れる場合は，well の後に置く。

2(1)Will you show me the way to the station?
　(2)He looks very tired. He must have worked too hard.
　(3)The story might［may］be true, but none of us believe it.
　(4)You had better not give your children snacks before meals.

8

(5) Both of them should share the information because they will attend the meeting.

(6) I asked you to buy ten ice cream cones, but could you please get one more?

(7) I would rather not drink the spicy juice.

(8) He doesn't have enough money to study abroad. He should have saved more money.

解説

2 (2) 「彼はとても疲れているようだ。あまりにも熱心に働きすぎたに違いない。」

(5) 「2人ともその会議に出るので，2人は情報を共有するはずだ。」

(6) Could[Would] you 〜? に please を付ける場合は，Could[Would] you please 〜? または Could[Would] you 〜, please? となる。

(7) would rather +動詞の原形〜「むしろ〜したい」。would rather で1つの助動詞の役割があるため，not を入れる場合は，rather の後に置く。

(8) 「彼は留学するための十分なお金がない。お金をもっと節約すべきだったのに。」

3 (1) Will[Can] you work

(2) shouldn't be difficult[hard]

(3) Should, wait for

(4) Would[Could] you raise

(5) would rather, than

(6) Should[Shall] I

解説

3 (2) 「〜ではないはずだ」は should not で表すことができる。

(5) would rather 〜 than ... 「…よりむしろ〜したい」

(6) 「(私が)〜しましょうか」は Should

[Shall] I 〜? で表すことができる。

4 (1) Can you tell me something important

(2) Will you look for the document

(3) should apologize for making us wait

(4) Could you send me the schedule by e-mail

(5) had better remember to give tips

(6) should have studied more for

解説

4 (3) apologize for 〜「〜のことで謝る」

(5) remember to 〜「忘れずに〜する」

STEP 3　まとめ問題

1 (1) Would[Could] you pass me the salt on the table?

(2) We cannot praise her too much.

(3) He must have taken the wrong road.

解説

1 (2) cannot +動詞の原形+ too の語順に注意。

(3) must have +過去分詞〜「〜したに違いない」

2 (1) We might catch the train

(2) had better watch your step

(3) There shouldn't be any mistakes [There should be no mistakes]

解説

2 (2) watch your step 「足元に気をつける」

(3) 「〜 があるはずだ[ないはずだ]」は There should[shouldn't] be 〜で表すことができる。

3 (1) Would[Could] you refrain from smoking here?

(2) You should have called the police sooner.

解説

3 (1) 相手に丁寧に依頼する文なので，Would

9

[Could] you 〜?で表す。助動詞の過去形を用いることで丁寧な表現となる。refrain from 〜「〜を控える」

(2)「〜すべきだった」は should have + 過去分詞〜で表す。

---

4 (例) I think that each of us should understand both the advantages and the disadvantages of social media to use it properly. I think one of the greatest advantages of social media is that it is very useful in times of disaster. That is because we can give and get important information through social media more easily. On the other hand, we must be careful about what we say on social media because it can hurt others when we freely express our opinions. We need to consider how our remarks may affect others at all times.

解説

4 ・「把握する」 → 「理解する」

・「いちばん〜な…の１つ」は one of the + 最上級＋名詞の複数形で表す。「(それは) 〜だからである」は That is because 〜で表す。

・「一方で(反対の意見を述べるとき)」は on the other hand を使う。express 〜「(考えなどを)述べる」

LISTENING

(1) I have no idea why you got angry
(2) You should have told me about it in advance
(3) I must have upset you
(4) I should be careful about it

10

LESSON 4	(pp.22-27)
完了形	

STEP 1 基本問題

❶ 1 (1) I have already arrived at the airport.

(2) Jane has visited Kyoto once.

(3) We have been busy since this morning.

2 私は本を借りるためにちょうど市の図書館に行ってきたところです。

解説

❶ 1 (1) 現在完了形・完了「〜したところだ,〜終えた」の文では already「すでに」や just「ちょうど」を伴うことが多い。

(2) 現在完了形・経験「〜したことがある」の文では once「1回」, twice「2回」, 〜 times「〜回」を伴うことが多い。

(3) 現在完了形・継続「(過去のある時点から)ずっと〜している」の文では since 〜「〜以来」や for + 期間の長さを表す語句「〜の間」を伴うことが多い。

2 have (just) been to 〜 は「(ちょうど)〜に行ってきたところだ」を表す。また, have been to 〜 は経験「〜に行ったことがある」も表す。

❷ 1 (1) When I got to the stadium, the game had already finished.

(2) I had never been on a plane before that.

(3) He said he had not eaten for three days.

2 私が返金を要求する前にお店は私にお金を戻しました。

解説

❷ 過去完了形は過去のある時点までに完了したこと, 経験したこと, 継続していたことを表す。

1 (2) never「一度もない」は完了形・経験でよく使われる。

❸ 1 (1) They have been making a lot of noise at the construction site all day.

(2) He had been running his own business until two years ago.

2 私たちはそのお客様を1時間待ち続けていますが, まだ着きません。

解説

❸ 現在完了進行形や過去完了進行形は現在または過去のある時点まで継続している[継続していた]ことを表す。

❹ 1 (1) The exams will have finished by next Wednesday.

(2) I will have known him for ten years before long.

2 その美術館は次の人が来館すると, 1,000人の訪問者を迎えたことになります。

解説

❹ 未来完了形は未来のある時点までに完了すること, 経験すること, 継続することを表す。

1 (1) by 〜「〜までに(完了して)」を表す。

STEP 2 実践問題

1 (1) ever (2) since (3) had

(4) has been raining (5) had been

(6) How long (7) had taken

(8) had had (9) will have been

(10) be

解説

1 (1) ever は「これまでに」を表し, 完了形の経験の文でよく使われる。

(3) Kathy が退職した時点までに継続していたことなので, 過去完了形にする。

(6) How long 〜? は期間をたずねる表現。How far 〜? は距離や程度をたずねる表

11

現。

(8) 旅行に行く機会があったのは Kate が私にたずねたときよりも前のことなので,過去完了形にする。

2 (1) She is good at English, so she has never gotten a bad score on her English exams.
(2) He hasn't been absent from work for two years.
(3) Someone had already repaired the machine before I tried.
(4) I recognized him at once since I had seen him many times.
(5) They had been married for twenty years when they decided to get a divorce.
(6) What have you been doing since you got here this morning?
(7) She will have been in Japan for three years next month.
(8) Will you have sent all the invitations by tomorrow?

解説
2 (1) never は「一度もない」を表し,完了形の経験の文でよく使われる。
(2)「2 年間」のように数を伴う「〜の間」と言う場合は for を使う。during の例:during my stay in London「私がロンドンに滞在する間」
(6) 今朝ここに来たときから今までし続けていることなので,現在完了進行形にする。
(8) 未来のある時点までに完了することなので,未来完了形にする。

3 (1) Have you, yet
(2) Has it, been, before
(3) had, by the time
(4) will have published
(5) more, than, had expected

(6) Will you have finished

解説
3 (1) yet は疑問文で「もう,すでに」を表す。
(3) by the time S V は「S が V するまで」を表す。by the time で 1 つの接続詞の働きをする。

4 (1) haven't seen him for the past
(2) has already been closed due
(3) told us that he had served
(4) haven't been getting enough sleep
(5) will have had enough experience when

解説
4 (1) the past 〜は「ここ最近〜」を表す。

STEP 3　まとめ問題

1 (1) They have not [haven't] heard the news yet.
(2) She has wanted to be a doctor since childhood.
(3) We will have studied English for six years by the time we graduate from high school.

解説
1 (1) yet は否定文で「まだ(〜ない)」の意味で,完了を表す文でよく使われる。
(2) since childhood「子どもの頃から(= since she was a child)」

2 (1) I will have climbed Mt. Fuji three times
(2) How long have they been growing
(3) I had never spoken to a foreigner

解説
2 (1)「明日」という未来の時点における経験なので,未来完了形で表す。
(3) 外国人に話しかけたことがないことは,

12

過去に高校に入学したときより前のこと
なので，過去完了形で表す。

3 (1) How many times have I told you the
same thing?

(2) All of them will have forgotten about
the rumor after[in] a while.

解説

3 (1) 現在までの経験なので，現在完了形の文
にする。「何度〜」は How many times 〜？
で表す。「あなたに同じことを言う」は
tell you the same thing と表せる。

(2) しばらく後になって完了することなの
で，未来完了形で表す。

4 (例) I'm going to imagine our society
in the near future. I'm sure that
technology will have advanced
further to make our lives more
convenient. One thing we can
anticipate is that we will be
able to make use of drones more
effectively. Drone delivery services
will be common, and many people
will be able to shop without going
to stores.

解説

4 ・I'm sure that 〜 .「（私は）きっと〜だ（と
思う），〜であることは間違いない。」

・make Ｏ Ｃ「Ｏ を Ｃ に す る」make our
lives more convenient「私たちの生活を
より便利にする」

LISTENING

(1) do you know what will happen in 2028

(2) 100 years will have passed

(3) You'll be excited if you can see his
original pictures

(4) I've heard that a lot of events were held

13

LESSON 5	(pp.28-33)
受動態	

STEP 1　基本問題

❶1(1) Kyoto is visited by many people every year.
(2) Is this seat taken by anyone?
(3) The book must be returned to the library by tomorrow.
2 その問題はトムによって対処されました。

解説
❶1(3) 助動詞の肯定文の受動態は助動詞 + be + 過去分詞となる。
2 動詞を含む熟語を使った受動態の文では動詞を過去分詞にしてそのまま使い，be dealt with となる。

❷1(1) The device is being introduced into a lot of hospitals.
(2) The matter has been observed by many scientists for years.
2 あなたは必要なものすべてを与えられましたか。

解説
❷1(1) 進行形の肯定文の受動態は be 動詞 + being + 過去分詞となる。

❸1(1) I was asked the way to the station by the woman.
(2) Your ID card must be shown to one of the staff members.
(3) Is Takashi called Taka for short?
2 その人たちは長時間，外で待たされました[待たされたままでした]。

解説
❸2 leave O C「O を C のままにしておく」の O が主語となった受動態。

❹1(1) It is often said that Japanese people are diligent.
(2) Is it believed that the story is true?
2 その国は 1 年中寒いと誤って信じられています。

解説
❹ It is said[believed] that S V = S is[are] said[believed] to V「S は V だと言われている[信じられている]」

STEP 2　実践問題

1(1) The sentences were translated into English by her.
(2) What language is spoken by the people in that country?
(3) The case was looked into by the police.
(4) The problem has to be handled by us carefully.
(5) He was reported to be a competent engineer by them.

解説
1(1) translate A into B「A を B に訳す」動詞の目的語の A を主語にして受動態を作る。
(2) What language を主語にして「何の言語がその国の人々によって話されていますか」とする。
(3) look into 〜「〜を綿密に調べる」
(4) have[has] to は助動詞と同じ扱いなので，have[has] to be + 過去分詞とする。

2(1) This article about the incident was found on the internet.
(2) Vegetables tend to be disliked by small children.
(3) She is known to everyone in town.
(4) Are the windows cleaned every day?

14

(5) It is thought that he is one of the best players in professional baseball.

(6) A lot of homework is given to us by the teacher every day.

(7) He was made to be a doctor by his parents.

(8) I was surprised to see English and Japanese written in her notebook.

解説

2 (1) by ～「～によって」はその行動(見つけた)を行ったものに使う。on the internet「インターネットで」

(2) tend to ～「～する傾向がある」「嫌われる(be disliked)傾向がある」とする。

(3) be known to ～「～に知られている」S is[are] known by ～「S は～でわかる」

(4) 毎日の習慣なので,現在形の受動態の疑問文にする。

(6) give A B「A に B を与える」の B が主語となった受動態は B is[are] given to A となる(= A is[are] given B)。

(7) make A B「A を B にする」の受動態は A is[are] made B[to be B]となる。

(8) be surprised to see[hear] ～「～を見て[聞いて]驚く」= be surprised at + 名詞

3 (1) is not taught

(2) Who was, taken by

(3) Are you interested in

(4) known as   (5) is made from

(6) are based on

解説

3 (2) This picture was taken by ～という文の～を Who にして文頭に置き,疑問文の形にする。

(3) be interested in ～[または動名詞～ing]「～(すること)に興味がある」

(4) be known as ～「～として知られている」

(5) be made from ～「～でできている」主語と原材料の質が変わらない場合は be made of ～を使う。

(6) be based on ～「～に基づく」

4 (1) Will an announcement be made to

(2) The project needs to be carried out

(3) The tradition has been passed down from

(4) It is well known that

(5) The building is referred to as

(6) All passengers are required to show

解説

4 (4) well known「よく知られている」

(5) refer to A as B「A を B と呼ぶ」A が主語になり,受動態となっている。

(6) be required to ～「～しなければならない,～するように義務付けられている」

STEP 3　まとめ問題

1 (1) How many e-mails are usually sent to you?

(2) When will the celebration party be held?

(3) We are not[aren't] allowed to take out the data.

解説

1 (2) will を使った受動態の疑問文にする。

(3) be allowed to ～「～することが許されている」

2 (1) if you want to be liked by them

(2) The clock was being repaired[fixed]

(3) The problem was caused by

解説

2 (2) 過去進行形の受動態にする。

(3) be caused by ～「～が原因である,～によって引き起こされる」

15

3 (1) I am tired[sick] of being scolded[told off].

(2) The result of the experiment was proved[proven] accurate by the team.

解説

3 (1) be tired[sick] of ～で「～に飽きている，うんざりしている」を表す。be tired from ～「～で疲れている」との違いに注意。「叱られる」は scold または tell off を受動態で表す。前置詞 of に続くので，being scolded[told off]となる。

(2) prove O C「OがCであることを証明する」を用いる。ここでは，O は the result of the experiment，C は accurate で，このOを主語にして受動態にする。

4 (例) I'm going to talk about something I want to try to improve my daily life. First, I want to start doing something I enjoy to relieve stress. I like flowers, so it would be nice to grow a variety of flowers on my balcony and enjoy looking at them every day. Second, I will be careful not to worry too much about trivial things and to be more relaxed in order not to get stressed out.

解説

4 ・be careful to[not to] ～「～するように[しないように]注意する。try to[not to] ～ でもよい。

LISTENING

(1) I heard you got heatstroke during soccer practice

(2) I've drunk plenty of water

(3) more than 100 people have already been taken to the hospital

(4) even though the heatstroke alert is not issued

LESSON 6	(pp.34-39)

比較①（比較級，最上級）

STEP 1　基本問題

❶1(1) The new team member is ten centimeters taller than me.

(2) I want to have a less expensive shirt.

(3) It's much warmer this year than last year.

2 彼の歌は確かにすばらしかったが，彼女のピアノ演奏の方がさらに良かった。

解説

❶1(1)「どれだけ（背が高い）」の部分は比較級の前に置く。

(2) less 〜は「より〜ではない」を表す。

(3) much「ずっと」や even「さらに」は比較級を強調する働きがある。

❷1(1) It's the most popular game among my classmates.

(2) We use the very best ingredients in our restaurant.

2 明日は私にとっては最も都合が悪いです。

解説

❷1(2) the very「まさに」は最上級を強調する働きがある。

2 the least 〜は「最も〜ではない」を表す。

❸1(1) She became more and more famous as an actor.

(2) There are no more than ten people in the village.

(3) It is not more than 500 meters from here to the station.

2 私は彼が内気なのでいっそう彼が好きです。

解説

❸2(all) the + 比較級 + for 〜は「〜だからそれだけいっそう」を表す。

❹1(1) I want to make the most of my ability.

(2) At least try to answer the first question.

2 彼女はとても若く見えたので，私は，彼女は多くみても30歳だと思いました。

解説

❹1(1) make the most of 〜は「（良い条件など）を最大限に活用する」を表す。

2 at most は「せいぜい，多くても（= not more than）」を表す。

STEP 2　実践問題

1(1) earlier　　(2) higher

(3) weaker and weaker　　(4) student

(5) the most　　(6) by far the most

(7) usual　　(8) the fastest

(9) best

解説

1(2)「どちらがより〜であるか」は Which is + 比較級〜で表す。

(3) 比較級 + and + 比較級は「ますます〜」を表す。

(4) 比較級 + than any other + 単数形...は「他のどの…よりも〜」を表す比較級を使った最上級の表現。

(5) one of the + 最上級 + 複数形は「最も〜な中の1つ」を表す。

(6) by far 最上級を強調する働きがある。the + 最上級で1つなので，by far は the の前に置く。

(7) than usual は「いつもより」を表す。

(8) the + 最上級〜 + in ...（場所・範囲を表す語句）で「…の中で最も〜」を表す。「〜（数を表す語句・複数）の中で」は of 〜を

17

(9) make the best of 〜は「(不利な事情・条件) を最大限に活用する，何とか切り抜ける」を表す。

2 (1) My mother is three years younger than my father.
(2) This river is about three times longer than that one.
(3) The more satisfied our customers are with our services, the happier we are.
(4) We have to solve the problem sooner or later.
(5) This software is by far the most commonly used of all.
(6) There is nothing worse than crowded trains in the morning.
(7) He is junior to me, but he is dependable.
(8) Voter turnout will be not[no] more than 30% because most citizens aren't interested in the election.

解説
2 (2) 「〜倍…である」という場合は，比較級の前に〜 times を置く。
(3) The ＋比較級〜，the ＋比較級...で「〜であればあるほど，より…だ」を表す。
(4) sooner or later は「遅かれ早かれ，いつかは」を表す。
(6) 後ろに than があるので，比較級にする。
(7) junior to 〜で「〜より年下の」を表す。senior「〜より年上の」，superior「〜より優れている」，inferior「〜より劣っている」などは to を付けて表す。
(8) 「ほとんどの市民がその選挙に興味がないので，投票率はせいぜい 30%[たった 30%]であろう。」

3 (1) easier to understand
(2) moves much more
(3) getting[becoming] cheaper and cheaper
(4) the second oldest
(5) least expected
(6) less difficult than

解説
3 (1) easy to understand「理解しやすい」
(4) the second ＋最上級〜は「2番目に〜な」を表す。
(5) この least に the は付かない。

4 (1) will be much smaller this month than
(2) nothing is more precious than
(3) is heavier than that one by
(4) more fish than we could eat
(5) call me at your earliest opportunity
(6) get an average score at best

解説
4 (3) by 〜は「〜の差で」という意味がある。
(5) at the[one's] earliest opportunity「できるだけ早い機会に，都合がつき次第」
(6) at best「良くても，せいぜい」

STEP 3　まとめ問題

1 (1) He looks better than before.
(2) It is[It's] the quickest way to learn a lot of[many] words.
(3) The harder we exercise[work out], the more weight we lose.

解説
1 (1) than before「以前よりも」
(3) The ＋比較級〜 , the ＋比較級...で表す。much を比較級 more にする。

2 (1) will make you feel better

18

(2) The most exciting moment was

(3) the last person to tell a lie

解説

2 (1) make O +動詞の原形～「O に～させる」の形を用いる。feel better「気分が良くなる」

(3) the last ～ to V …[who V …]は「最も…しそうでない～」を表す。

---

3 (1) No one understands the system better than he does.

(2) Arrive at[Get to] the airport at least thirty minutes before your departure time.

解説

4 (1) no one「だれも～ない」を主語にし，「彼よりも～をよく理解している人はだれもいない」という比較級の文で表せる。well の比較級 better を用いる。

(2) 命令文で表す。at least「少なくとも」

---

4 (例) Our group researched the food situation in the world. Japan's food self-sufficiency rate based on calories is 38%. It was more than[over] 70% in 1965. We made many more farm products at that time, but production has gradually decreased due to the increase of cheaper imports from other countries. Canada is one of the countries that has one of the highest food self-sufficiency rates, and the rate is about seven times higher than[as high as] that in Japan. The reason for this is that Canada has many large farmlands and the population is small for the land area.

解説

4 ・「～以上」は more than[over] ～で表す。

・「～の割に」は for ～で表す。

LISTENING

(1) Much more electricity is made from solar power

(2) it's better for Japanese schools to have solar panels

(3) Schools need more and more electricity

(4) We can make the most of sunlight in that way

19

LESSON 7 (pp.40-45)
比較②(同等比較，倍数比較など)

STEP 1 基本問題

❶ 1 (1) This picture is as expensive as that one.
(2) Your garden is large, but mine is as large.
(3) I get up as early as my mother.
2 あなたのお姉さん[妹さん]は振る舞いが優雅ですが，あなたの振る舞いも同じくらい優雅です。

解説
❶ 1 (2) as large の後は as your garden が省略されている。

❷ 1 (1) They are about twice as old as I am.
(2) His income is three times as high as mine.
2 このノート型パソコンの重量は従来のものの3分の2です。

解説
❷ 1 「～倍の…だ」という場合は as ... as の前に twice または～ times を置く。

❸ 1 (1) He is not so much a writer as a journalist.
(2) Come back as soon as you can.
(3) As many as three thousand flowers are planted in the field.
2 私は動くことができる限り，その工場で働きたいです。

解説
❸ 1 (1) not so much A as B(= B rather than A)は「A というよりもむしろ B」を表す。
(2) as ～ as S can(= as ～ as possible)は「(S が)できるだけ～」を表す。
(3) as many as ～は「～もの多くの」を表す。

2 as long as S V は「S が V する限り(条件)」を表す。

❹ 1 (1) I will leave everything to the younger generation from now on.
(2) Whether you have received a higher education is not important.
2 それらの高級ホテルは1人あたり1泊5万円以上かかります。

解説
❹ younger generation「若い世代」，higher education「高等教育」，better-class「高級な，上流の」は特定のものとの比較ではなく，漠然と程度の高低を示す表現である。

STEP 2 実践問題

1 (1) as well as　(2) half as large as
(3) one third as heavy
(4) as well as　(5) you can
(6) not so much, as

解説
1 (1)(a)「プロのように」
(b)「プロと同様に上手に」
(2)(a) half the size of ～「～の半分の大きさ」
(3)(a) three times my weight「私の3倍の重さ」
(4) not only A but also B(= B as well as A)「A だけでなく B も」

2 (1) The musician has as many fans as Steve.
(2) I should have studied as hard as he did.
(3) The cost of living in this country is many times as high as that in my home country.
(4) We need a few more people to carry these desks.
(5) I walked as far as Tokyo Station.

20

(6) The number of customers was one and a half times as large as that of the previous year.

解説

2 (1) as + 形容詞 + (a) + 名詞 + as の語順となる。

(2) hardly は「ほとんど〜ない」という意味。

(3) cost of living「生活費」

(4)「もういくつかの」は数字 + more(= another + 数字)の語順になる。a few more people = another few people

(5) as far as 〜は「(距離が)〜の所まで」を表す。

(6) 1.5 倍は one and a half times となる。

3 (1) as bitter as
(2) as[so] young as, looks
(3) three times as deep as
(4) as early[soon] as
(5) as, as ever[before]
(6) higher animal

解説

3 (1)「こんな苦いコーヒー」→「これと同じくらい苦いコーヒー」

(2) not as[so] 〜 as ...「…ほど〜ではない」

(4) as early as 〜は「早ければ〜に、早くも〜に」を表す。

(5) as 〜 as ever は「相変わらず〜」を表す。

(6) higher animal「高等動物」

4 (1) is as good as finished
(2) is as quick to work as
(3) so stupid as to make
(4) as sensible a girl as any
(5) as rude a person as ever lived
(6) As far as I'm concerned

解説

4 (1) as good as 〜は「〜も同然で」を表す。

(2) be quick to 〜「〜するのが速い」

(4) as 〜 as any は「だれにも劣らず〜」を表す(= as sensible as any other girl)。

(5) as 〜 as ever lived は「極めて〜、この上なく〜」を表す。

(6) as far as S + be 動詞 + concerned は「S に関する限り」を表す。

STEP 3　まとめ問題

1 (1) No dictionary is as useful as that one.
(2) Would you speak as slowly as she does?
(3) As far as I know, she is still a college [university] student.

解説

1 (3) as far as S know(s) は「S が知る限りでは」を表す。

2 (1) as many boxes as you need
(2) as near[close] to our destination as possible
(3) for larger men

解説

2 (1) as many boxes as you need[like]「あなたが必要な[好きな]だけの箱」

(2) near[close] to 〜「〜に近い」

(3)「体の大きい男性」→「体のより大きい男性」

3 (1) No student gets scolded by teachers as much as he does.
(2) Our baby sleeps nearly twice as long as we do every day.

解説

3 (1) no + 単数名詞を主語にした as 〜 as ... の文は「…ほど〜の—はない」の意味で、実質的には最上級と同じ内容になる。「叱られる」は get scolded(get を使った受動態)で表せる。

(2) nearly twice で「2 倍近く」の意味。こ

21

れを as long as ～の前に置いて，「～の2倍近く長く」とする。

---

4 (例) I searched for information on the internet about how much smartphones are used in Japan. According to a survey, the rate of women and men aged between 15 and 79 who have a smartphone is 94% in 2022, which is about four times as many as ten years ago. As of 2022, approximately 70% of people in their seventies have a smartphone. This means that a lot of elderly people in Japan still don't have a smartphone. I think it is important to have a society where people who don't have a smartphone can live as comfortably as people who do.

解説

4・「…の約4倍の～である」は about four times as ～ as …で表す。

・live comfortably「快適に[不自由なく]暮らす」「～と同様に不自由なく」は as comfortably as ～で表す。

LISTENING

---

(1) On the other hand, that in Australia is above 90%

(2) The turnout in Australia is about twice as high as that in France

(3) they have a great influence on the government

(4) the younger generation gets interested in politics

LESSON 8
動名詞
(pp.46-51)

STEP 1 基本問題

❶ 1 (1) Visiting a new place is exciting.
(2) My hobby is putting puzzles together.
(3) Hiroshi likes taking pictures of trains.
2 私は他国で人々に日本語を教えることに興味があります。

解説
❶ 1 動名詞(動詞の〜ing形)は「〜すること」を意味し,主語,補語および目的語になる。
2 in などの前置詞の後は名詞,代名詞または動名詞を置く。

❷ 1 (1) We were worried about being fired.
(2) He is proud of having won the race.
2 私は高く評価されすぎて[買い被られて]困惑しています。

解説
❷ 1 (1) 受け身の動名詞は being +過去分詞となる。
(2) 「勝った」のは「誇りに思う」ことより前のことなので,完了形の動名詞 having +過去分詞となる。

❸ 1 (1) Would you mind my leaving the window open?
(2) I am sure of his taking over my business.
2 私たちは彼の若い年齢のため,彼が私たちのグループに入るのを反対した。

解説
❸ 1 (1) Would you mind A(所有格または目的格)〜ing? は「Aが〜してもいいですか」を表す。Aは動名詞の意味上の主語である。

❹ 1 (1) The proposal is worth considering.
(2) There is no telling what will happen tomorrow.
(3) I feel like having a cup of coffee after each meal.
2 彼は決して考えを変えないだろう。彼を説得しようとしても無駄だ。

解説
❹ 1 (1) A is worth 〜ing は「Aは〜する価値がある」を表す。
(2) There is no 〜 ing は「〜することはできない」を表す。
(3) feel like 〜 ing は「〜したい気がする」を表す。
2 It is no use[good] 〜 ing は「〜しても無駄だ」を表す。

STEP 2 実践問題

1 (1) Living (2) Keep (3) dancing
(4) talking (5) posting (6) trying
(7) having said (8) being called
(9) working (10) say

解説
1 (2) 動名詞だと文の意味が通らない。原形にして命令文にする。
(3) enjoy 〜 ing「〜するのを楽しむ」
(4) stop 〜 ing「〜するのをやめる」, stop + to 不定詞〜「〜するために止まる」
(5) remember 〜 ing「〜したことを覚えている」, remember + to 不定詞〜「〜することを覚えている,忘れずに〜する」
(6) How about 〜 ing?「〜してはどうですか」
(9) get[be] used to 〜 ing「〜することに慣れる[慣れている]」
(10) What do you say to 〜 ing?「〜するのはどうですか」

23

2 (1) Looking at the picture makes me happy.
(2) Be kind to everyone whoever she or he is.
(3) I stopped to take a deep breath because I came in a hurry.
(4) I hope to see her again in the near future.
(5) I will never forget visiting Egypt last summer.
(6) Having made the event a success together is a good memory.
(7) This card is used to unlock the door of the laboratory.
(8) Please excuse me for being late.

解説

2 (4) hope + to 不定詞〜「〜したいと望む」
(5) forget 〜 ing「〜したことを忘れる」, forget + to 不定詞「〜するのを忘れる」
(6)「イベントを成功させた」のは過去のことなので, 完了形の動名詞とする。
(7)「鍵を開けるために」を表すため, to 不定詞とする。
(8) 前置詞 for の後は名詞または動名詞を置く。

3 (1) starting[beginning], continuing
(2) finished repairing[fixing]
(3) denied having stolen
(4) before having[eating]
(5) his offer being
(6) When it comes to

解説

3 (2) finish 〜 ing「〜し終わる」
(3) deny 〜 ing「〜したことを否定する[していないと言う]」バッグを盗んだとされるのはさらに過去のことなので, 完了形の動名詞とする。
(6) when it comes to 〜 ing「〜ということ

においては」

4 (1) are growing flowers and drawing landscapes
(2) should have practiced making the presentation
(3) admitted to having run out of
(4) your purchase prior to placing an order
(5) cannot help doing something when
(6) On arriving at a final decision

解説

4 (2) practice 〜 ing「〜することを練習する」
(4) prior to 〜 ing「〜する前に」
(5) cannot help 〜 ing「〜せずにいられない」
(6) on 〜 ing「〜するとすぐに」

STEP 3　まとめ問題

1 (1) Writing a play is very interesting for me.
(2) We look[are looking] forward to welcoming the new employees.
(3) There is no point (in) regretting it now.

解説

1 (2) look forward to 〜（名詞または動名詞）「〜を楽しみに待つ」
(3) There is no point (in) 〜 ing「〜しても無駄だ」

2 (1) Thank you for giving us the wonderful[great] opportunity
(2) is good at getting
(3) We are busy (in) preparing for

解説

2 (1) Thank you for 〜 ing「〜してくれてありがとう」
(3) be busy (in) 〜 ing「〜するのに忙しい」

24

3 (1) I was aware of his[him] avoiding me.

(2) She left without saying goodbye to me.

解説

3 (1) be aware of ～で「～に気づいている」を表す。avoid「避ける」は of のあととなので動名詞にするが，意味上の主語である「彼」は主文の主語「私」とは異なるので，avoiding の前に his または him を置く。

(2) without ～ ing「～せずに」

4 (例) This book was written by Mr. Tetsu Nakamura, a Japanese doctor. It tells us about what he and the people around him did after he went to Pakistan to work at a hospital. Dr. Nakamura saw people suffering from famine, and he began digging wells to support their livelihoods. Moreover, he devoted himself to constructing irrigation canals for a secure supply of water. As a Japanese, I am proud of him for having worked hard for so long to make others happy, no matter where they are from.

解説

4 ・devote oneself to ～ ing「～することに献身する」

・be proud of ～「～を誇りに思う」him[his]は動名詞の意味上の主語で，「(彼が)長年働いた」のは過去のことなので，完了形の動名詞となる。

LISTENING

(1) Thank you for lending me this book

(2) educating girls is as important as educating boys

(3) after being treated at a hospital

(4) This book tells us the importance of education

25

LESSON 9
to 不定詞

(pp.52-57)

STEP 1　基本問題

❶1 (1) To study English is enjoyable.
　(2) My dream is to work for people all over the world.
　(3) Do you want to travel into space in the future?
　2 その英語の長い手紙を日本語に翻訳するのはそれほど簡単ではない。

解説

❶1 to 不定詞〜は「〜すること」を表すことができ，主語や補語，目的語となる。
　2 It は to 不定詞以下を指す。

❷1 (1) Kyoto has many places to visit.
　(2) Please give me something to drink.
　2 私は試験で自分のすべての解答を確認する（ための）十分な時間がなかった。

解説

❷ to 不定詞〜は名詞を修飾して「〜する（ための）」を表すことができる。

❸1 (1) I went to the library to borrow a book.
　(2) I awoke to find that no one was at home.
　2 私は彼女が病気から回復しつつあることを聞いてうれしいです。

解説

❸1 (1) to 不定詞〜は「〜するために」という目的を表すことができる。
　(2) awake to find 〜「目が覚めると〜だとわかる」
　2 感情を表す形容詞（〜）+ to 不定詞 ...は「…して〜である」を表す。

❹1 (1) I want to have him look at my PC.
　(2) His jokes made us laugh.
　(3) I heard someone call my name in the distance.
　2 あなたがピアノを動かすのを手伝いましょうか。

解説

❹1 (1) have O + 動詞の原形〜「O に〜させる，してもらう」
　(2) make O + 動詞の原形〜「O に〜させる」
　(3) hear O + 動詞の原形〜「O が〜するのを耳にする」
　2 help O + 動詞の原形（または to 不定詞）〜「O が〜するのを手伝う，〜するのに役立つ」

STEP 2　実践問題

１(1) something cold to drink　(2) want
　(3) to　(4) seeing　(5) to attend
　(6) to keep　(7) how to change
　(8) in order not to　(9) to follow
　(10) make

解説

１(1) something + 形容詞 + to 不定詞 の語順となる。
　(2) want 〜「〜が欲しい，必要である」
　(4) look forward to 〜 ing「〜するのを楽しみにする」
　(5) forget + to 不定詞〜「（これから）〜するのを忘れる」
　(6) tell O + to 不定詞〜「O に〜するように言う」
　(7) how + to 不定詞〜「〜する方法」
　(8) in order + to 不定詞〜は「〜するために」という目的を表す。否定語は to の前に置く。
　(9) make + A + 動詞の原形の受動態は A is [are] made + to 不定詞となる。

26

2 (1) It is impossible to finish reading the report in one day.

(2) We found it difficult to get used to a new environment.

(3) I was sad to hear that she would be leaving our office.

(4) Remember to thank them for their cooperation.

(5) I want you to train new staff members for me today.

(6) I tried to get him to change his behavior.

(7) He spent two hours repairing his bike.

(8) How long does it take to get to the hospital by bus?

解説

2 (2) find it + 形容詞〜 + to 不定詞 ...「…することは〜だとわかる［思う］」it は to 不定詞以下を指す。

(4) remember + to 不定詞〜「（これから）〜することを覚えている，忘れずに〜する」

(5) want O + to 不定詞〜「O に〜してほしい」

(6) get O + to 不定詞〜 = have O +動詞の原形〜

(7) spend + 時間 + 〜 ing「〜するのに時間を費やす」

(8) it takes + (人) +時間 + to 不定詞〜「(人が)〜するのに時間がかかる」

3 (1) can't［cannot］afford to

(2) something［anything］to say

(3) no time to lose

(4) To tell the truth

(5) never to

(6) have nothing to do with

解説

3 (1) can't［cannot］afford + to 不定詞〜「〜

する余裕がない」

(4) to tell the truth「実を言うと」

(5) never + to 不定詞〜「(その結果)二度と〜しない」

(6) have something［nothing］to do with 〜「〜と関係がある［ない］」

4 (1) the first Japanese baseball player to play in

(2) am sorry to keep you waiting

(3) has a great desire to

(4) going abroad to have new experiences

(5) What made him decide to

(6) All you have to do is

解説

4 (5) What makes O +動詞の原形〜？「何が O に〜させるのか」=「なぜ O は〜するのか」

(6) all S have to do is + to 不定詞〜「S は〜しさえすればよい」

STEP 3　まとめ問題

1 (1) Who was the first person to come up with the idea?

(2) I am［I'm］relieved to find that you are safe.

(3) My son is old enough to take care of himself.

解説

1 (3) 〜 enough + to 不定詞 ...「…するのに十分〜だ」

2 (1) The goal［aim］of this class is to make［help］you

(2) I heard about the plan to

(3) seem to be different from

解説

2 (1) 補語に to 不定詞を用いる。

27

(2) 形容詞的用法の不定詞が前の名詞を修飾
    する。

(3) seem + to 不定詞〜「〜と思われる」

3 (1) I found it convenient to pay money
       using my smartphone.
   (2) I was asked to stay[remain] in the
       company.

解説

3 (1) find it + 形容詞〜 + to 不定詞 ...「…す
        ることは〜だとわかる［思う］」の形。it
        は to 不定詞以下を指す。
    (2) ask O + to 不定詞の目的語が主語になっ
        て受動態となった形。

4 (例) I want to introduce two games that
        we can enjoy easily. You may have
        seen them on TV or on the internet.
        We don't need to pay or prepare
        special devices for the games. One
        of them is the "No English" game.
        You cannot use English words
        during the game. You may find
        it difficult to talk without using
        English words. The other one is
        the "Wet Towel Roulette" game.
        Players wring a towel in turn, and
        the one who cannot squeeze a drop
        of water out of it is the loser. How
        about trying a game that is not a
        video game?

解説

4 ・need + to 不定詞〜「〜する必要がある」
   ・in turn「順番に」
   ・How about 〜 ing?「〜してはどうですか」

LISTENING

(1) the players moved really fast and
    smoothly

(2) Is it possible for them to follow the
    same rules

(3) Thanks to the different devices to play
    with

(4) Now I want to watch parasports too

28

LESSON 10
分詞
(pp.58-63)

STEP 1　基本問題

❶1 (1) The sleeping baby is lovely.
(2) Whose is the horse running over there?
2 最前列に座っている男性が見えますか。

解説

❶1 現在分詞は修飾される名詞が「〜する，している」を表し，現在分詞１語で修飾する場合は名詞の前に，現在分詞が語句をともなう場合は名詞の後ろにつける。

❷1 (1) There are some broken windows in the building.
(2) Please show me the pictures taken by him.
2 カレンが受け取った小包はどこだろうか。

解説

❷1 過去分詞は修飾される名詞が「〜される」を表し，過去分詞１語で修飾する場合は名詞の前に，過去分詞が語句をともなう場合は名詞の後ろにつける。

❸1 (1) I saw Tim walking around the station.
(2) Did you hear your name called?
(3) Keep the machine running for a while.
2 私は運転免許証を更新してもらわなければなりません。

解説

❸1 (1)(2) see[hear] O ＋現在分詞[過去分詞]〜「O が〜している[される]のを見る[耳にする]」
(3) keep O ＋現在分詞[過去分詞]〜「O が〜している[される]状態にしておく」

2 get[have] O ＋過去分詞〜「O を〜してもらう」

❹1 (1) Talking with my friend, I noticed that he was worried about something.
(2) Seen from a distance, he looked younger.
(3) Judging from my experience, she hasn't been able to use all her talent.
2 その生徒たちは目を輝かせながら私の話を聞いた。

解説

❹1 (1) When I was talking 〜を分詞構文にするには，接続詞 when をとり，主語が主節と同じ場合はとり，動詞を分詞にする。分詞構文は「〜するとき」を表すことができる。
(2) When[If] he was seen 〜を分詞構文にした形。
(3) judging from 〜「〜から判断すると」
2 with O ＋現在分詞[過去分詞]〜「O を〜して[されて]」

STEP 2　実践問題

1 (1) the man talking　(2) stolen bag
(3) read　(4) visiting　(5) falling
(6) injured　(7) used　(8) irritated
(9) folded　(10) Written

解説

1 (6) injure 〜は「〜にけがさせる」で，「(人などが)けがしている」という場合は injured となる。
(8) irritate 〜は「〜をいらつかせる」で，「(人が)いらついている」という場合は irritated となる。
(9)「腕」は「折りたたまれる」ので，過去分詞となる。

29

2 (1) I'm worried about the crying boy.

(2) She has a car made in China.

(3) Our English teacher often tells us interesting stories.

(4) Ten people, including Kate and me, are participating in the event.

(5) I went to the dentist to have my tooth filled.

(6) Generally speaking, Japanese people tend not to reveal their intentions.

(7) Tired of his work, he patiently continued it.

(8) Not having met with him for many years, I didn't recognize him immediately.

解説

2 (3) interest 〜 は「〜を興味づける」で，「(話などが)興味深い」という場合は interesting となる。

(4) including 〜「〜などの，〜を含めた」

(5) have a tooth filled「歯に詰め物をしてもらう」

(6) generally speaking「一般的に言って」

(7) Although he was tired 〜 を分詞構文にした形。

(8) 分詞構文で否定語は分詞の前に置く。

3 (1) man standing

(2) Interested students

(3) was seen buying[purchasing]

(4) thanking, for

(5) Weather permitting

(6) Taking, into consideration[account]

解説

3 (2) 「(人が)興味がある」という場合は interested。

(3) see O +現在分詞〜「O が〜しているのを見る」の受動態。

(5) weather permitting「天気がよければ」

(6) taking 〜 into consideration[account]
(= considering 〜)「〜を考慮して」

4 (1) The man wearing a mask and repairing a car

(2) was covered with fallen leaves

(3) was so excited by the news that

(4) to have our plans accepted

(5) Not knowing what to do

(6) Never leave small children playing

解説

4 (2) fallen leaves「落ち葉」

(3) excite 〜 は「〜を興奮させる」で，「(人が)興奮している」は excited となる。

(6) leave O +現在分詞[過去分詞]〜「O を〜のままにしておく，〜の状態にしておく」

STEP 3 まとめ問題

1 (1) The woman giving a presentation is a doctor.

(2) Don't give us confusing information.

(3) She was running with her hair blowing in the wind.

解説

1 (1) 「している」という能動の意味を表すので，give を現在分詞にして woman の後ろに置く。

(2) confuse 〜 は「〜を混乱させる」で，「(情報などが)混乱させるような」は confusing となる。

(3) with O +現在分詞[過去分詞]〜「O を〜して[されて]」の形。「髪」は「なびく」という能動の関係なので，blow は現在分詞となる。

2 (1) the book written by her

(2) This is the most boring TV drama

30

解説

2 (1) 「彼女によって書かれた本」と表す。write を過去分詞にして book の後ろに置く。

(2) bore ～は「～を退屈にさせる」で，「(何かが人を)退屈にさせる」は boring になる。

---

3 (1) Walking in a strange city, I happened upon an acquaintance.

(2) It starting to rain, so we took a taxi.

(3) Because[Since] I had[have had] a similar experience, I understand your feelings.

解説

3 (2) 分詞構文では主語が主節と違う(it と we)場合は，主語を残す。

(3) 分詞構文の having + 過去分詞は主節よりも時制が前ということなので，接続詞を使った文では過去形または現在完了形にする。

---

4 (例) This is the News Today Show. Here is today's news. Have you ever seen monkeys passing nearby? We have recently reported a few times that monkeys have appeared in the city, and that a monkey was seen in Sakaemachi today. The police spent more than five hours trying to catch the monkey after receiving a call, but lost sight of it in the end. Fortunately, no one was attacked by the monkey. Never go close to monkeys when you see them.

解説

4 ・「サルが通り過ぎていくのを見る」は see monkeys passing とする。

・「サルに襲われた～」は～ attacked by the monkey とする。

LISTENING

(1) I saw a lot of oil flowing from a ship

(2) it'll do harm to the environment around the area

(3) Generally speaking, it takes at least 100 days to remove the oil

(4) the sea will be clean again soon

31

LESSON 11　　　　　　　(pp.64-69)
関係詞①（関係代名詞）

STEP 1　基本問題

❶1 (1) Did you take part in the conference which was held yesterday?
(2) The woman who he married is a lawyer.
(3) Tell me what is needed.
2 あなたは1週間前に借りた本を返しましたか。

解説

❶1 (1) which は先行詞が人以外の主格または目的格の関係代名詞。
(2) who は先行詞が人の主格または目的格（= whom）の関係代名詞。
(3) what はそれ自体に先行詞（もの，こと）を含む関係代名詞。
2 that は先行詞が何であるかにかかわらず使え，主格または目的格となる。

❷1 (1) The boy whose mother is a teacher also wants to become a teacher.
(2) The house whose roof is red is mine.
2 私は本社がアメリカにある会社に勤めている。

解説

❷ whose は先行詞が何であるかにかかわらず使うことができ，所有格となる。

❸1 (1) All of us trust him, who never tells a lie.
(2) The family, who moved from abroad, got used to living here easily.
(3) This is Ms. Imai, whom I have known since I was a child.
2 彼の作品の一つは数百年前に書かれたものだが，いまだに人気がある。

解説

❸ 関係代名詞の非制限用法（カンマ＋関係代名詞）は先行詞や先行する文の一部または全部を補足的に説明する用法。

❹1 (1) We will welcome whoever wants to join our club.
(2) Report whatever occurs here to me.
(3) Whoever has the responsibility, all of us should think of a solution.
2 あなたがどれを選んでも，大差はない。

解説

❹1 (1)(3) whoever ～「～する人はだれでも」「だれが～しても」
(2) whatever ～「するものは何でも」「何を～しても」
2 whichever ～「～するものはどれでも」「どれを～しても」

STEP 2　実践問題

❶ (1) what　　(2) that　　(3) that
(4) whose　　(5) what　　(6) to whom
(7) that　　(8) with which　　(9) which
(10) anyone

解説

❶ (1) what you said「あなたが言ったこと」
(5) what he was「過去の彼」
(6) to は spoke の後でも，前に置いて「to ＋関係代名詞の目的格」でもよい。
(7) 先行詞に人と人以外の両方が含まれる場合は that を使う。
(8) 「前置詞＋関係代名詞の目的格」では that は使えない。
(9) which は he could speak English を受けている。that に非制限用法はない。
(10) 「どなたか私の声が聞きづらい場合は，私に知らせてください」

32

2 (1) I want to ask for the opinion of someone who is familiar with the law.

(2) I looked up what I wanted to know in the encyclopedia.

(3) The report mentions something that is important to our lives.

(4) This is the picture of which Allen is proud.

(5) I learned the procedure from him, which was a mistake.

(6) He, whose father is the president of the company, got promoted.

(7) Whoever wins first prize in the contest, it matters little to me.

(8) What is more, they revealed an unexpected finding.

解説

2 (4) be proud of 〜「〜を誇りに思う」の of を関係代名詞の前につける。

(5) この which はカンマの前全体を受ける。

(7) whoever は単数扱い。

(8) what is more「さらに」

3 (1) which[that] I want

(2) whose brother

(3) Whatever[What] has, has

(4) what is called[what we call]

(5) of which

解説

3 (3) whatever は単数扱い。

(4) what is called[what we call]「いわゆる」

4 (1) that I have ever been to

(2) her talent, which I think is great

(3) made me what I am

(4) whose meanings many Japanese people don't know

(5) Whatever course you choose to take

(6) Whichever of you tries the method

解説

4 (2) which is great に I think を挿入した形。

(3) what I am「今の私」「私の周りの人たちが私を今日の私にした」

(6) whichever of 〜「〜のうちのどちらが…でも」

STEP 3 まとめ問題

1 (1) The section to which I belong is on the third floor.

(2) He missed the train that left[leaves] Hiroshima at ten.

解説

1 (1) belong to 〜で「〜に所属する」なので, to which(to that は不可)のように to をつけ忘れないように。

2 (1) which I found impossible

(2) who is not[isn't] usually late for work

解説

2 (1) which は to improve working conditions を受ける。find O C「O が C だとわかる」の O に入る部分が関係代名詞となって前にくる。

3 (1) Whoever comes to see me, I will not [won't] see them.

(2) He was selected as the new president, which I expected.

解説

3 (1)「だれが〜しても」という副詞節では whoever を主語にする。whoever は単数扱いであることに注意。

(2)「彼が〜に選ばれた」は, select O as 〜「O を〜に選ぶ」の受動態で表せる。その後ろに, 前の文の内容を受ける非制限用法の関係代名詞 which を続けて「それは私が予想した」と表す。which の前にカン

33

4 (1) 私は会議に参加したが，会議の間，私は居眠りした。

(2) あなたがどんな言い訳を思いついても，彼女を納得させられないだろう。

them

(2) "fair trade" products are a little more expensive

(3) Those who make them are paid properly for their work and time

(4) buying them will help those people

解説

4 (1) which の先行詞は the meeting。

(2) whatever「どんな…を〜しようとも」

5 (例) We are looking for students who want to participate in the work experience program in kindergartens. Participants will be divided into groups, each of which will visit one kindergarten. Whoever is interested can join the program, but the number of participants is limited to fifteen students. Fill out the form and describe what you want to do with the children, such as playing or drawing pictures with them, and submit it. You can bring books or prepare pictures to tell a story. How about having a good time with children?

解説

・「〜したい生徒」は students who[that] want to 〜とする。

・each of which の which の先行詞は groups。

・「興味のある人はだれでも」は Whoever is interested とする。この部分が文の主語となる。

・「あなたがしたいこと」は what you want to do とする。

LISTENING

(1) I've read a book which is written about

34

LESSON 12
関係詞②（関係副詞）

(pp.70-75)

STEP 1 基本問題

❶ 1 (1) It snowed heavily on the day when I was born.
(2) This is the park where we used to play baseball.
(3) He didn't explain the reason why he was late.
2 機械がどのように動くか見せてくれますか。

解説

❶ 1 (1) when は時を表す語句を先行詞として説明を加えるための関係副詞。
(2) where は場所・場合を表す語句を先行詞として説明を加えるための関係副詞。
(3) why は理由を表す語句を先行詞として説明を加えるための関係副詞。

❷ 1 (1) They arrived at my house at seven, when the party started.
(2) I like Paris, where I have lived for a year.
2 彼は先週までアメリカに滞在して，それからカナダに向かった。

解説

❷ 関係副詞の前にカンマを置く用法は時間や場所について補足的な説明をする。
1 (1) , when は「（そして）それから」という意味を表す。
(2) , where は「（そして）そこで」という意味を表す。

❸ 1 (1) I have a meal at home whenever it is possible.
(2) My son follows me wherever I go.
2 知らない英単語を見つけたときはいつでも，辞書で調べなさい。

解説

❸ 1 (1) whenever ～「～するときはいつでも」
(2) wherever ～「～するところはどこでも」

❹ 1 (1) However late you are, be sure to call me.
(2) Whenever an opportunity arises, I'm prepared to exceed expectations.
(3) Wherever you live, I wish you good luck.
2 その植物はどこで育てられるとしても，よく成長するだろう。

解説

❹ 複合関係副詞は譲歩の意味を表すことができる。
1 (1) however ～は「どんなに～でも」。後の語順に注意。
(2) whenever ～「いつ～しようとも」
(3) wherever ～「どこで～しようとも」

STEP 2 実践問題

1 (1) There was a time when I was good at running.
(2) Linda works at the company where I worked before.
(3) I have no idea why he wants to quit his job.
(4) Wherever she appears, many people gather around her.
(5) This book includes how we make good coffee.

解説

1 (5) 抜けている主語(we)を補って，「私たちがおいしいコーヒーをいれる方法」とする。

2 (1) You should be careful of the timing when you tell the truth.
(2) I want to go to the place where people

35

can relax.

(3) I want to see how she shows her leadership.

(4) That is (the reason) why he recovered so soon.

(5) We climbed to the top of a mountain, where we camped.

(6) Come tomorrow, when I will have more time.

(7) I will take you wherever you want to visit.

(8) Whenever I come here, I see someone I know.

解説

2 (1) 関係副詞 when は前置詞＋関係代名詞に置きかえることができる。

(3) 関係副詞 how は the way in which に置きかえることができる。

(4) 関係副詞 why は the reason for which に置きかえることができる。That is why ～「そういう理由で～」

(5) 関係副詞 where の非制限用法は，カンマ＋ and there で言いかえることができる。

(6) 関係副詞 when の非制限用法は，カンマ＋ and then で言いかえることができる。

(7) to any place you want to visit は「あなたが行きたいところはどこへでも」。wherever は副詞なので，to は不要になる。

(8) every time ～「～するときはいつでも」

3 (1) job where　　(2) Morning is when

(3) That is why　　(4) This is how

(5) wherever you　　(6) however hard

解説

3 (2) 関係副詞 when はその中に時を表す先行詞を含む用法がある(= the time when)。

(3) That is why ～「そういう訳で[だから]～」

(4) This is how ～「このようにして～」

4 (1) come when you will regret it

(2) cases where our efforts aren't rewarded

(3) There is no particular reason why

(4) how we should deal with

(5) whenever he rides in vehicles

(6) However you look at it

解説

4 (6) however S V「S が V するどんな方法でも」

STEP 3　まとめ問題

1 (1) I was about to leave at seven, when I got a call.

(2) This is (the place) where the car accident happened.

解説

1 (2) 関係副詞 where はその中に場所を表す先行詞を含む用法があるため，the place は省略可。

2 (1) from where we are sitting

(2) How those animals get their food

解説

2 (1) from where ～「～するところから」

(2) 関係副詞 how はその中に先行詞を含み，「～する方法」の意味を表す。

3 (1) I will never forget the time when I first met you.

(2) However difficult it is to realize your dream, you should not[shouldn't] give up easily.

解説

3 (1) 「初めてあなたと会ったとき」は the time を先行詞として，関係副詞 when を使う。

(2) 「～することがどんなに難しくても」は however を使って表す。it is so difficult to ～ の so difficult を however difficult

4 (1) 彼女がパーティーに来なかった理由は
スケジュールが合わなかったからです。

(2) 私はどこへ行こうが，常に周囲に注意
を向けています。

解説

4 (1) 関係副詞 why はその中に理由を表す先行
詞を含む用法がある(= the reason why)。

5 (例) I'm going to tell you why I recommend Switzerland as a good tourist site. When you think of Switzerland, you may recall the beautiful scenery seen in a popular Japanese animation series, but the actual scenery of Switzerland is much grander and more beautiful. Switzerland has lovely cities like Zurich, where we can feel comfortable. Switzerland is relatively safe and has a good public transportation system, so it's a wonderful country for tourists to enjoy their trip.

解説

5 ・「なぜ(私が)〜するのか」は why I 〜で表す。

・「〜を感じることができる…」は , where we can feel 〜で表す。

LISTENING

(1) however strongly they wish to

(2) I can hardly imagine the situation where children cannot study

(3) all children have a right to go to school wherever they are

(4) we should tell our friends about this problem

LESSON 13	(pp.76-81)
仮定法	

STEP 1 　基本問題

❶ 1 (1) If he practiced harder, he could be a strong player.
　(2) If I were you, I would accept the offer.
　2 だれかが彼の連絡先を知っていれば，私たちは彼にそのことを知らせることができるのに。

解説

❶ 仮定法過去は現在の事実と異なる仮定を表す。if 節では動詞の過去形，be 動詞は were を使う。主節は助動詞の過去形＋動詞の原形とする。

❷ 1 (1) If you had been there at that time, you could have seen the performance.
　(2) If I had left home a little earlier, I might have been on time for the train.
　2 彼がその過程を詳しく説明していたら，私たちは彼をもっと支援できたのに。

解説

❷ 仮定法過去完了は過去の事実と異なる仮定を表す。if 節は had ＋過去分詞となる。主節は助動詞の過去形＋ have ＋過去分詞となる。

❸ 1 (1) The attempt wouldn't be successful without their collaboration.
　(2) I started at once, otherwise I would have been late.
　(3) I could have answered all the questions with more time.
　2 テレビで取り上げられたその医者なら，あなたの病気を治せるだろう。

解説

❸ 1 (1) 仮定法で if 節の代わりに without ～で「～がなければ［なかったら］」を表す。
　(2) otherwise ＋仮定法の主節～で「（カンマの前を受けて）～でなければ～だろう［だったろう］」を表す。
　(3) 仮定法で if 節の代わりに with ～で「～があれば」を表す。
　2 仮定法では主語が if 節の代わりをすることがある。

❹ 1 (1) If it were not for tests at school, I would never study.
　(2) If it had not been for you, no one would have known what to do.
　(3) It's high time you made a decision.
　2 あなたは薬を飲む時間です。

解説

❹ 1 (1) if it were not for ～で「もし～がなければ」を表す。
　(2) if it had not been for ～で「もし～がなかったら」を表す。
　(3) It is (high または about) time ＋ S ＋過去形～で「～してもいい頃だ」を表す。

STEP 2 　実践問題

1 (1) learned　　(2) were
　(3) had been　　(4) otherwise
　(5) would trust　　(6) it were not for
　(7) had eaten

解説

1 (5) If 節は過去のことなので仮定法過去完了，主節は現在のことなので仮定法過去となる。
　(7) I wish S ＋過去形～［had ＋過去分詞～］で「S が～すれば［していたら］なあ」を表す。

38

2 (1) If I had enough money, I would[could] buy the new type of smartphone I want.

(2) If you had not[hadn't] followed the doctor's advice, you would not [wouldn't] be healthy now.

(3) If it were not for[there were not] an alarm clock, I would be late for school every day.

(4) If it had not been for the funding, we could not have carried out the project.

(5) If she should resign as chairperson, who on earth could take over her position?

(6) I wish I could afford to pay for you.

(7) I don't like to be treated as if[as though] I were a child.

解説

2 (5) 仮定法の if 節の were to[should]は「万一（起こる可能性がほとんどないこと）」という意味を表す。

(6) 「あなたの分を払う余裕がないことが残念だ」→「あなたの分を払う余裕があればなあ」

(7) as if[as though] S ＋過去形〜[had ＋過去分詞〜]で「Sがあたかも〜である[であった]かのように」を表す。

3 (1) were asked

(2) Had it not been[If it hadn't been]

(3) wish, had made

(4) But for

(5) Were I

解説

3 (2) If it had not been for は If を使わない場合，倒置が起こり，Had it not been for となる。

(4) but for 〜は「〜がなければ[なかったら]」

を表す(＝ without 〜)。

(5) If I were は If を使わない場合，倒置が起こり，Were I となる。

4 (1) how would you want to change

(2) I had had more experience

(3) If only I were more

(4) Should you have any questions

(5) surprised as if she had seen

(6) Had I known you were in the hospital

解説

4 (2) have more experience は「もっと経験がある」で，仮定法過去完了の If 節なので had had 〜となる。

(3) If only S ＋過去形〜[had ＋過去分詞〜]で「Sが〜であればなあ[であったならなあ]」を表す(＝ I wish)。

(4) If you should 〜で If をとると倒置が起こり，Should you 〜となる。

(6) If I had 〜で If をとると倒置が起こり，Had I 〜となる。

STEP 3　まとめ問題

1 (1) If you were good at speaking in public, I would like you to take my place.

(2) Although he knew nothing[didn't know anything] about the subject, he talked as if[as though] he were an expert.

解説

1 (1) 「（人）に〜してもらいたいのだが」は would like ＋人＋ to 〜で表す。

2 (1) If it had not been for[Without, But for]

(2) as if[as though] it (had) happened to someone else

39

解説

2 (2) as if[as though]以下は，主節と同じ時であれば仮定法過去，それ以前と考えられれば仮定法過去完了で表す。

---

3 (1) If it had not[hadn't] rained heavily yesterday, we could use the baseball field today.

(2) I wish I had been kinder to him.

解説

3 (1) If節は過去のことなので仮定法過去完了，主節は現在のことなので仮定法過去となる。

(2) 過去の事実と異なる願望は，I wish S + had + 過去分詞～で表す。「もっとやさしい」は kind の比較級で表す。

---

4 (1) 20年前なら，だれもそんなことは信じなかっただろう。

(2) スマートフォンがなかった時代に生まれていたなら，私たちは不便を感じただろう。

解説

4 (1) 副詞句(Twenty years ago)が If 節の代わりをしている。

(2) 分詞構文(Born ～ smartphones)が if 節の代わりをしている。

---

5 (例)One child dies of hunger every ten seconds in the world. Wars and regional conflicts have a huge impact on vulnerable children. On the other hand, more than six million tons of food is disposed of in Japan every year. Although you may not take it seriously, would you throw away food you can still eat if hungry children were in front of you? I wish people around the world shared food without wasting it.

解説

5 ・③「あなたはお腹をすかせた子どもたちが～食べ物を捨てるだろうか」は仮定法過去で表す。

・④「（現在）～していればいいのにと思う」は I wish S + 過去形～で表す。

LISTENING

(1) These talking robots are controlled by artificial intelligence

(2) If it were not for AI

(3) we should not depend too much on it

(4) It's high time we humans learned to live with AI

LESSON 14　(pp.82-87)
特殊構文

STEP 1　基本問題

❶1(1) In case I'm late, start without me.
　(2) As long as we are here, we are safe.
　(3) Even if he knows little about the subject, he speaks as if he does.
2 私の兄はまだ学生であるにもかかわらず，私の学費を払うために働いている。

解説
❶1(1) in case S V「S が V する場合，S が V するのに備えて」
　(2) as long as S V ～「S が V する限り」条件を表す。
　(3) even if S V「たとえ S が V しても」
2 even though S V「S が V するにもかかわらず，たとえ S が V しても」

❷1(1) Her parents supported her so that she could realize her dream.
　(2) My father was so weak that he couldn't walk without a stick.
　(3) Given that she has contributed greatly to the company, she should get promoted.
2 2 つのグループは合意に達したので，事態は好転するだろう。

解説
❷1(1) so that S(＋助動詞)＋V「S が V するように」
　(2) so ～ that ...「とても～なので…だ」
　(3) given that S V「S が V することを考慮して」
2 now that S V「もう S は V なので」

❸1(1) His courage enabled him to start a new business.
　(2) Her cold prevented her from going to school.
　(3) What made you break your promise?
2 現代の通信技術により，私たちはより簡単に在宅勤務ができます。

解説
❸1(1) S enable O ＋ to 不定詞～「S のおかげで O は～できる」
　(2) S prevent O from ～ ing「S のせいで O は～できない」
　(3) What makes O ＋動詞の原形～?「なぜ O は～するのか[何が O に～させるのか]」

❹1(1) That dress does look good on you.
　(2) It is this book that I want to read.
2 それを食べるには，お湯を入れるだけでよい。

解説
❹1(1) do[does, did]は助動詞として動詞を強調する用法がある。
　(2) 強調構文は強調したい部分を It is[was]と関係詞(that など)の間に置く。
2 All S have[has] to do is ＋ to 不定詞～「S は～するだけでよい」

STEP 2　実践問題

1(1) long　　(2) go
　(3) leave　　(4) to tell

解説
1(1) as long as S V「S が V する限り」は条件を表す。
　(2) この did は助動詞なので，あとには動詞の原形がくる。
　(4) S allow O ＋ to 不定詞～「S により O は～できる」

41

2 (1) In case you miss the train, please contact me as soon as possible.

(2) Unless you are rude to him, he will respond to your request.

(3) We need to use electric devices to some extent, whether we like it or not.

(4) He is so tall a man that I asked him to get me the item on the top shelf.

解説

2 (1) in case S V などの副詞節では，未来のことは現在形で表す(will は使えない)。

(2) unless S V「S が V しない限り」

(3) whether S V (or not)「S が V であろうとなかろうと」

(4) so ＋形容詞＋ a[an] ＋名詞の語順になる。

3 (1) We should prepare food and water for a few days in case there is[in case of] an emergency.

(2) I got up early so that I would[could, can] submit the report earlier than my classmates.

(3) All we can do is to wait for him to come back.

(4) It was at that shop that he bought the bike.

(5) His pride did not[didn't] allow him to admit what he did.

解説

3 (1) for (an) emergency「非常用に」→「非常時に備えて」

(2) in order ＋ to 不定詞～「～するために」目的を表す。

(3) all S can do is ＋ to 不定詞～「S は～するしかない」

(5) due to ～「～のため（理由）」

4 (1) As far as　(2) Even if[though]

(3) Whether, or not　(4) do come

(5) It is because　(6) reminds, of

解説

4 (1) as far as S know(s)「S が知る限り」

(5) Because you stay up late at night, you are sleepy ～という文で，because you stay up late at night を強調した構文。

(6) remind O of ～「O に～を思い出させる」

5 (1) in case any players got injured

(2) as long as I live

(3) unless she is too tired

(4) whether they are important or trivial [trivial or important]

(5) such a great movie that I

解説

5 (5) such a ＋形容詞＋名詞＋ that ～の語順になる。

STEP 3　まとめ問題

1 (1) All we have to do is to follow her instructions.

(2) It is not she but he that[who] is responsible.

(3) Ten minutes' walk from the station brought me to the museum.

解説

1 (1) all S have[has] to do is to 不定詞～「S は～するだけでよい」

(2) not she but he を強調するために It is と that の間に置く。

(3)「駅から 10 分間の徒歩が私を博物館に連れて来た」とする。

2 (1) Even if the next seat is empty[isn't taken]

(2) so that she would[could] be[become] a lawyer

42

(3) Now that you have graduated

(3) That's why he didn't eat my curry

(4) so that we can live happily and peacefully

解説

2 (2) that 節は，弁護士になるのは過去の時点から見た未来のことなので would または could を使う。

3 (1) As long as you are happy, I don't worry about you.

(2) The heavy rain prevented us from practicing baseball on the field.

解説

3 (1) 「～でありさえすれば」＝「～である限り」as long as ～で表す。

(2) S prevent O from ～ ing 「S のせいで O は～できない」の文で，S を the heavy rain，O を us にする。

4 (例) When we hear the word Bulgaria, the first thing we think of is yogurt. In Bulgaria, yogurt is made from sheep's milk as well as cow's milk. Bulgarians not only eat yogurt as it is but also make salad dressing and soup with it. Furthermore, there are many kinds of cheese in Bulgaria, and Bulgarians eat cheese almost every day. Given that many Bulgarians live long lives, maybe we should try eating a little more yogurt and cheese.

解説

4 ・「ブルガリア人は長寿の人が多いので～」は Given that ～ 「～であることを考慮に入れると」を使って表すことができる。

LISTENING

(1) Even if your dish were delicious

(2) they don't eat pork for religious reasons

43

| 2年の総合問題 | (pp.88-93) |

第1回　LESSON 1～5

1 (1) belongs　　(2) was
(3) will be working　　(4) is expected
(5) must　　(6) might as well
(7) had you been looking　　(8) held
(9) left　　(10) be made up for

解説

1 (1) belong は状態動詞なので，進行形にはできない。
(2) at that time「その時，当時」は過去を表す。
(3) by this time next year「来年の今頃には」は未来の一時点なので，未来進行形(will be ～ ing)にする。
(4) be expected + to 不定詞～「(主語)が～すると期待[予想]される」
(5) must ～には「～に違いない」という意味がある。
(6) might as well + 動詞の原形～「～した方がいい」
(7) 「それを見つけた」という過去の一時点まで進行していたことは，過去完了進行形(had been ～ ing)で表す。
(8) hold ～で「(会などを)行う」で，「行われる」とするために受動態とする。be held = take place
(9) leave O C「O を C のままにしておく」
(10) make up for ～「(損失などを)埋め合わせる」the loss(その損失)が主語なので，受動態にする。

2 (1) We were having dinner when the phone rang.
(2) The league season begins in April every year.
(3) You had better not underestimate her abilities.

(4) We cannot emphasize the importance of understanding each other too much.
(5) I was happy to see him yesterday because I hadn't seen him in a long time.
(6) I haven't completed the report yet, though I have to submit it tomorrow morning.
(7) The driver's carelessness was thought to be the cause of the accident.
(8) I was told to stop by my grandparents' house.

解説

2 (1) 「電話が鳴ったときに夕食を食べていた」ということなので，過去進行形にする。
(2) 毎年の習慣的行事なので，現在形にする。
(3) had better ～「～した方がいい」は，2語で1つの助動詞として扱われるので had better not となる。
(4) cannot ～ too much「～してもし過ぎることはない」
(5) 「昨日」という過去の一時点まで彼に会っていなかったということなので，過去完了形にする。
(6) 現在，完了していないことを表すので，現在完了形にする。
(7) be thought + to 不定詞～「(主語)が～する[～である]と思われる」
(8) be told + to 不定詞～「～するように言われる」

3 (1) He is[He's] always thinking of food. [All he thinks of is food.]
(2) I would rather stay home than go shopping.
(3) The students looked as if they were about to fall asleep.

44

解説

3(1) be always ～ing「～ばかりしている」

(2) would rather +動詞の原形～(than +動詞の原形 ...)「(…するよりも)むしろ～したい」

(3) be about + to 不定詞～「まさに～しようとしている」

4(1) he was arriving here at six

(2) will have won ten games

(3) Would you wait here

解説

4(1) 進行形は予定されている未来を表すことができる。往来発着を表す動詞で使うことが多い。

(2) 未来において完了することなので，未来完了形(will have +過去分詞)で表す。

5(1) あなたはその計画をもっと慎重に進めるべきだった。

(2) 彼女は公衆衛生の専門家として有名です。

解説

5(1) should have +過去分詞～「～すべきだった(のにしなかった)」

(2) be known as ～「～として有名だ」

第2回 LESSON 6 ～ 10

1(1) much better than

(2) as[so] much as[no less than]

(3) after finishing, homework

(4) something[anything] to read

(5) glad[happy] to be

(6) with, running

解説

1(1) much は比較級を修飾して「ずっと～」という意味を表す。

(2) as much as ～「～もの(多くの)」不可算名詞とともに使う。可算名詞の場合は as

many as ～。no less than ～はどちらの場合にも使える。

(3) ここで使う after は前置詞なので，あとは名詞または動名詞が続く。

(4) something[anything] + to 不定詞～「～するためのもの」疑問文でも肯定の答えを期待する場合は something を使う。

(5) 感情を表す形容詞～ + to 不定詞 ...「…して～だ」

(6) with O +分詞～「O が～して」my child と run は能動の関係なので，running となる。O と～が受け身の関係では過去分詞を使う(例：with my eyes closed「目を閉じて」)。

2(1) was less interesting than the first half

(2) as many questions as you can

(3) don't like me going out

(4) found it difficult to put

(5) had my mother take care of

(6) not live to see his work completed

解説

2(1) less は形容詞や副詞を修飾して「(…ほど)～ではない」を表す。

(2) as ～ as S can[possible]「できるだけ～」

(3) like O ～ing[to 不定詞]～「O に～してほしい，O が～するのを好む」O は動名詞[to 不定詞]の意味上の主語。

(4) find it ～ + to 不定詞 ...「…するのは～だと思う，わかる」

(5) have O +動詞の原形～「O に～させる，してもらう」have O +過去分詞～「O を～される，してもらう」

(6) see O +過去分詞～「O が～されるのを見る」

3(1) The population of this city is one and a half times larger than that of my city.

45

(2) It will stop raining soon.

(3) Seen from the sky, the city is beautiful.

解説

3(1)「～倍の…だ」は～ times（2 倍は twice）＋比較級＋ than［as ＋原級＋ as］で表す。

(2)「～し終わる」は stop ～ ing で表す。stop ＋ to 不定詞～「～するために止まる」

(3) When the city is seen from the sky を分詞構文にするには，接続詞 When をとり，the city は主節の主語と同じなのでとり，Being seen ～となるが，being は省略可なので Seen from the sky となる。

4(1) more than four participants

(2) the young(er) generation of people are not responsible for

(3) is worth hearing

解説

4(1) no more than ～「わずか～」（＝ only ～）

(2) the young(er) generation「若い世代」

(3) worth ～ ing「～する価値がある」

5(1) 私はこのチャンスを最大限利用したい。

(2) すべてを考慮すると，それはいい買い物［取引］です。

解説

5(1) make the most of ～「（有利な状況・条件を）最大限利用する」，make the best of ～「（不利な状況・条件を）最大限利用する」

(2) All things considered「すべてを考慮すると」

第 3 回　LESSON 11 ～ 14

1(1) what interests　　(2) whose walls

(3) whenever we are

(4) however busy　　(5) That's why

(6) were［was］not

解説

1(1) 関係代名詞 what はそれ自体に先行詞を含み「～するもの，こと」を表す。

(2) whose は人，物および事を先行詞とする所有格の関係代名詞の用法があり，あとに先行詞に関連する名詞がくる。

(3) whenever S V「S が V するときはいつも」

(4) however ～（形容詞または副詞）S V「S がどんなに～でも，S がどんなに～に V しても」

(5) That's why S V「そういう訳で S は V する」

(6) 仮定法過去は If S ＋過去形（be 動詞は原則 were），S ＋助動詞の過去形＋動詞の原形の形で，現在の事実と異なることを仮定する。

2(1) the apartment that I will rent

(2) where we can park a car

(3) might not have missed the train

(4) If it were not for

(5) As long as this condition persists

(6) was so polite a man that

解説

2(1) that は人，物および事を先行詞とする主格または目的格の関係代名詞の用法がある。

(2) where は場所・場合を表す語句を先行詞としてそれを説明するための関係副詞。

(3) 仮定法過去完了は If S ＋過去完了（had ＋過去分詞），S ＋助動詞の過去形＋ have ＋過去分詞の形で，過去の事実と異なることを仮定する。

(4) If it were not for ～は仮定法過去の If 節で，「もし～がなければ」を表す。

(5) as long as S V は「S が V する限り」という条件を表す。as far as S V「S が V する限りでは」は程度を表す。as far as

I know「私が知る限り(範囲)では」

(6) so 〜 that ...「とても〜なので…だ」so ＋形容詞＋ a［an］＋名詞の語順になる（＝ such a［an］＋形容詞＋名詞）。

---

3 (1) Give the booklet to whoever is interested.

(2) He speaks to us as if［as though］he were our teacher.

(3) What brought you here?

解説

3 (1) whoever 〜「〜する人はだれでも」単数扱いであることに注意。

(2) as if S ＋過去形〜［過去完了形〜］「まるで S が〜する［した］かのように」

(3)「何があなたをここに連れて来たのですか」とする。

---

4 (1) which may be boring at the beginning

(2) when I was not［wasn't］at home

(3) you have to do is to

解説

4 (1) カンマ＋関係詞は先行詞や先行する文の全体または一部について補足的に説明する用法である。この which は The movie を先行詞とする主格の関係代名詞である。

(2) カンマ＋関係副詞 when は「(そして)その時」という意味を表す。

(3) All S have［has］to do is ＋ to 不定詞〜「S は〜するだけでよい」

---

5 (1) 私は彼にそのような愚かな質問をしなければよかった。

(2) 突然の予定変更で，彼はパーティーに出席できなかった。

解説

5 (1) I wish S ＋過去形〜［過去完了形〜］]「S が〜すればいいのに［していればよかった

のに]」事実に反する願望を表す。

(2) prevent O from 〜 ing「O が〜するのを妨げる」「彼の予定の突然の変更が，彼がパーティーに出席するのを妨げた」とする。

47

APPLAUSE
ENGLISH LOGIC AND EXPRESSION II
ワークブック
解答・解説

開隆堂出版株式会社
東京都文京区向丘 1-13-1

BE

3 日本語の意味に合うように，空所に適切な語を入れましょう。

(1) この学校ではフランス語は教えられていません。

French _____ _____ _____ in this school.

(2) この写真はだれによって撮られましたか。

_____ _____ this picture _____ _____?

(3) 人前で自己表現することに興味がありますか。

_____ _____ _____ _____ expressing yourself in public?

(4) 彼は SF 小説を書く作者として知られています。

He is _____ _____ an author who writes science fiction novels.

(5) この肉は 100％大豆から作られています。

This meat _____ _____ _____ 100% soybeans.

(6) 彼女の行動は綿密な計画に基づいています。

Her actions _____ _____ _____ her careful planning.

4 日本語の意味に合うように，(　　　)内の語句を並べかえましょう。

(1) 私たちに詳細を知らせるために発表はなされるのですか。

(made / will / to / be / an announcement) inform us of the details?

_____

(2) そのプロジェクトはすぐに実行される必要があります。

(carried / to / needs / out / the project / be) quickly.

_____

(3) その伝統は代々伝えられてきました。

(has / from / down / been / the tradition / passed) generation to generation.

_____

(4) 適量のワインが体に良いことはよく知られています。

(is / that / well / it / known) a moderate amount of wine is good for your health.

_____

(5) その建物はキャンパス内では「文系タワー」と呼ばれています。

(referred / the building / as / is / to) "Bunkei Tower" on campus.

_____

(6) 乗客の皆様の切符を拝見いたします。

(show / required / all / are / to / passengers) their tickets.

_____

31

LESSON 5
受動態

教科書 pp.36-41

STEP 3 まとめ問題

1 ( )内に与えられた語句を必要なら形を変えて使い，英文を完成させましょう。

(1) ふだん，あなたにどのくらいの E メールが送られますか。(send)

_____

(2) 祝賀パーティーはいつ開かれますか。(the celebration party / hold)

_____

(3) 私たちはそのデータを持ち出すことを許されていません。(allow / take out)

_____

2 日本語の意味に合うように，英文を完成させましょう。

(1) 人から好かれたいなら，人に親切にしなさい。

Be kind to people _____.

(2) 私がその部屋に入ったとき，その時計は修理されているところでした。

_____ when I entered the room.

(3) その問題はコミュニケーションの欠如が原因で引き起こされました。

_____ a lack of communication.

3 次の日本語を英語に直しましょう。

(1) 私は叱られるのにうんざりです。

_____

(2) その実験結果はチームによって正確であることが証明されました。

_____

4 次の３つの項目を入れて，かよさんがこれから習慣にしたいことについての英文を作ってみましょう。

① これから，日々の生活をよりよくする(improve)ために行いたいことについて話したい。

② まず，ストレスを緩和するために，自分が楽しいと思うことを始めたい。花が好きなので，ベランダで(on my balcony)いろいろな花を育て，毎日それを見て楽しむのがよいだろう。

③ また(Second)，ストレスにやられ(stress out)ないために，ささいな(trivial)ことを気にしすぎ(worry too much)ず，もっとリラックスするよう心がけたい。

_____
_____
_____
_____

🔊 LISTENING

会話を聞いて，(1)～(4)の内容を書きとりましょう。

熱中症で倒れた拓をエイミーが心配しています。(*A*: Amy　*T*: Taku)

A: Taku, are you OK? (1)_____.

T: Thanks. I'm getting better. (2)_____,
and it's cool here in the nurse's office.

A: Have you ever gotten heatstroke before?

T: No. It's the first time. I've never dreamed of it.

A: It is said that (3)_____ this
month because of heatstroke.

T: We should be careful (4)_____.
I'll take a break more often next time.

(1) _____
(2) _____
(3) _____
(4) _____

LESSON 6
比較①（比較級，最上級）

教科書 pp.44-49

STEP 1 基本問題

❶ 比較級を用いた表現

1 日本語の意味に合うように（　）内の語句を並べかえ，文全体を書き直しましょう。

(1) その新しいチームメンバーは私より 10 cm 背が高い。

The new team member (than / ten centimeters / is / taller) me.

_____

(2) 私はもっと安いシャツが欲しいです。

I want to have (shirt / a / expensive / less).

_____

(3) 昨年より今年の方がずっと暖かい。

It's (much / this year / warmer / than) last year.

_____

2 次の英文を日本語に訳しましょう。

His song was certainly great, but her piano performance was even better.

_____

❷ 最上級を用いた表現

1 日本語の意味に合うように（　）内の語を並べかえ，文全体を書き直しましょう。

(1) それは私のクラスメートの間で最も人気のあるゲームです。

It's (popular / most / game / the) among my classmates.

_____

(2) 当レストランではまさに最高の食材のみを使っています。

We use (very / best / the) ingredients in our restaurant.

_____

2 次の英文を日本語に訳しましょう。

Tomorrow is the least convenient for me.

_____

❸ 比較級を用いたさまざまな表現

1　日本語の意味に合うように（　　　）内の語句を並べかえ，文全体を書き直しましょう。

(1) 彼女は俳優としてますます有名になりました。

She became (more / more / famous / and) as an actor.

_____

(2) その村には 10 人しかいません。

There are (more / no / ten / than) people in the village.

_____

(3) ここから駅までせいぜい 500 メートルです。

It is (500 meters / more / than / not) from here to the station.

_____

2　次の英文を日本語に訳しましょう。

I like him all the better for his shyness.

_____

❹ 最上級を用いたさまざまな表現

1　日本語の意味に合うように（　　　）内の語を並べかえ，文全体を書き直しましょう。

(1) 私は自分の能力を最大限に活用したい。

I want to (the / make / of / most) my ability.

_____

(2) 少なくとも最初の質問には答えてみてください。

(at / to / least / try) answer the first question.

_____

2　次の英文を日本語に訳しましょう。

She looked so young that I thought she was at most 30 years old.

_____

LESSON 6

比較① （比較級，最上級）

教科書 pp.44-49

STEP 2　実践問題

1 (　　)内から適切な語句を選びましょう。

(1) I got up (more early / earlier) than my mother this morning.

(2) Which is (high / higher), this tower or the building over there?

(3) The wind was getting (weaker and weaker / weakest and weakest).

(4) He is taller than any other (student / students) in his school.

(5) She is one of (most / the most) reliable researchers.

(6) The place is (the by far most / by far the most) beautiful I have ever seen.

(7) Today's task took less time than (usual / usually).

(8) Kazuyo runs (faster / the fastest) in my class.

(9) We made the (most / best) of a bad situation.

2 例にならって下線部の誤りを訂正し，文全体を書き直しましょう。

(例) My father always keep my promise. → My father always keeps his promise.

(1) My mother is younger than my father three years.　（語順をかえる）

_____

(2) This river is about three longer than that one.

_____

(3) More satisfied our customers are with our services, happier we are.

_____

(4) We have to solve the problem soon or late.

_____

(5) This software is the most by far commonly used of all.　（語順をかえる）

_____

(6) There is nothing worst than crowded trains in the morning.

_____

(7) He is junior than me, but he is dependable.

_____

(8) Voter turnout will be more than 30% because most citizens aren't interested in the election.

_____

_____

3 日本語の意味に合うように，空所に適切な語を入れましょう。

(1) 彼女の説明は私のよりもわかりやすい。

Her explanation is ＿＿＿＿＿ ＿＿＿＿＿ ＿＿＿＿＿ than mine.

(2) 彼女は他のスタッフよりずっと動きが速い。

She ＿＿＿＿＿ ＿＿＿＿＿ ＿＿＿＿＿ quickly than the other staff members.

(3) コンピュータはどんどん安くなっています。

Computers are ＿＿＿＿＿ ＿＿＿＿＿ ＿＿＿＿＿ ＿＿＿＿＿.

(4) これが町で 2 番目に古いお寺です。

This is ＿＿＿＿＿ ＿＿＿＿＿ ＿＿＿＿＿ temple in the city.

(5) それは私たちが最も予想していなかったことです。

That's something we ＿＿＿＿＿ ＿＿＿＿＿.

(6) その試験は前の試験ほど難しくありません。

The exam is ＿＿＿＿＿ ＿＿＿＿＿ ＿＿＿＿＿ the previous one.

4 日本語の意味に合うように，（　　）内の語句を並べかえましょう。

(1) 今月は先月よりずっと予算が少ないでしょう。

The budget (smaller / be / than / much / will / this month) last month.

＿＿＿＿＿＿＿＿＿＿＿＿＿＿＿＿＿＿＿＿＿＿＿＿＿＿＿＿＿

(2) 親にとって，我が子ほど大切なものはありません。

For parents, (than / is / precious / more / nothing) their children.

＿＿＿＿＿＿＿＿＿＿＿＿＿＿＿＿＿＿＿＿＿＿＿＿＿＿＿＿＿

(3) このバッグの方があれより 500g だけ重い。

This bag (one / is / by / than / heavier / that) 500 grams.

＿＿＿＿＿＿＿＿＿＿＿＿＿＿＿＿＿＿＿＿＿＿＿＿＿＿＿＿＿

(4) 私たちは 2 ～ 3 日で食べきれないほどの魚をもらいました。

We got (more / could / we / fish / eat / than) in a few days.

＿＿＿＿＿＿＿＿＿＿＿＿＿＿＿＿＿＿＿＿＿＿＿＿＿＿＿＿＿

(5) 都合がつき次第，お電話いただけますか。

Would you (at / call / your / opportunity / me / earliest)?

＿＿＿＿＿＿＿＿＿＿＿＿＿＿＿＿＿＿＿＿＿＿＿＿＿＿＿＿＿

(6) 彼はその試験では良くても平均点しか取れないでしょう。

He will (an average / best / score / at / get) on the exam.

＿＿＿＿＿＿＿＿＿＿＿＿＿＿＿＿＿＿＿＿＿＿＿＿＿＿＿＿＿

LESSON 6

比較①（比較級，最上級）   教科書pp.44-49
STEP 3 まとめ問題

1 (　　)内に与えられた語を必要なら形を変えて使い，英文を完成させましょう。

(1) 彼は以前よりも元気そうに見えます。(good)
___

(2) それがたくさんの単語を覚えるいちばん速い方法です。(quick / learn)
___

(3) 懸命に運動するほど，体重が減ります。(hard / much)
___

2 日本語の意味に合うように，英文を完成させましょう。

(1) この薬を飲めば，あなたは気分が良くなるでしょう。
　　This medicine _____.

(2) 最も興奮させる瞬間は，彼女が舞台に現れたときでした。
　　_____ when she appeared on stage.

(3) 彼は決して嘘をつくような人間ではありません。
　　He is _____.

3 次の日本語を英語に直しましょう。

(1) 彼ほどそのシステムのことをよく理解している人はいません。
___

(2) 少なくとも出発時刻の30分前に空港に到着してください。
___

4 あるグループが各国の食糧事情について調べた次の内容の英文を作ってみましょう。

　　私たちのグループは世界の食糧事情(food situation)を調べてみました。日本の食料自給率(food self-sufficiency rate)はカロリーに基づくと38％です。1965年には70％以上ありました。当時はずっと多くの農産物(farm products)を作っていましたが，外国からの安い輸入品の増加により，生産量(production)が徐々に減っていきました。最も食料自給率が高い国の1つがカナダで，日本の約7倍です。カナダは広大な農地(farmlands)が多く，面積(land area)の割に人口が少ないからです。

_____
_____
_____
_____

🔊 LISTENING

会話を聞いて，(1)〜(4)の内容を書きとりましょう。
　ロンは，先生と太陽光パネルについて話しています。(*R:* Ron　*T:* Teacher)

R: My elementary school in the U.S. had solar panels, but I seldom see them on school buildings in Japan.

T: No. (1)_____ in the U.S. than in Japan.

R: In my view, (2)_____.

T: Why do you think so?

R: (3)_____. We use computers in class, and we also use air conditioners a lot.

T: That's true. (4)_____. What's more, solar power doesn't harm the environment.

(1) _____
(2) _____
(3) _____
(4) _____

LESSON 7

比較②（同等比較，倍数比較など）

教科書 pp.50-55

STEP 1 基本問題

❶ 同等比較

1 日本語の意味に合うように（　　　）内の語句を並べかえ，文全体を書き直しましょう。

(1) この絵画はあの絵画と同じくらい値段が高い。

This picture (as / is / expensive / as) that one.

_____

(2) あなたの庭は広いが，私の庭も同じくらい広いです。

Your garden is large, but (large / is / mine / as).

_____

(3) 私は毎朝，母と同じくらい早く起きます。

I get up (early / my mother / as / as).

_____

2 次の英文を日本語に訳しましょう。

Your sister behaves elegantly, but you behave as well.

_____

❷ 倍数比較

1 日本語の意味に合うように（　　　）内の語を並べかえ，文全体を書き直しましょう。

(1) その人たちは私の2倍程の年齢です。

They are (about / old / as / twice) as I am.

_____

(2) 彼の収入は私の3倍です。

His income is (high / as / times / three) as mine.

_____

2 次の英文を日本語に訳しましょう。

This laptop is two thirds as heavy as conventional ones.

_____

40

❸ 原級を用いたさまざまな比較表現

1　日本語の意味に合うように（　　　）内の語句を並べかえ，文全体を書き直しましょう。

(1) 彼は作家というよりむしろジャーナリストです。

He is (much / a journalist / so / as / not / a writer).

_____

(2) できるだけ早く戻ってきてください。

Come back (as / can / you / soon / as).

_____

(3) その野原には 3,000 本もの花が植えられています。

(three thousand / many / as / flowers / as) are planted in the field.

_____

2　次の英文を日本語に訳しましょう。

As long as I can move, I would like to work in the factory.

_____

❹ 特殊な比較表現

1　日本語の意味に合うように（　　　）内の語を並べかえ，文全体を書き直しましょう。

(1) 今後はすべて若い世代に任せます。

I will leave everything (generation / younger / to / the) from now on.

_____

(2) あなたが高等教育を受けたかどうかは重要ではありません。

Whether you (higher / have / a / education / received) is not important.

_____

2　次の英文を日本語に訳しましょう。

The better-class hotels charge more than fifty thousand yen per night per person.

_____

LESSON 7
比較② (同等比較，倍数比較など)
教科書 pp.50-55
STEP 2 実践問題

1 (a)と(b)の文がほぼ同じ意味になるように，空所に適切な語を入れましょう。

(1) (a) He plays the guitar like a professional.

    (b) He plays the guitar ＿＿＿＿＿ ＿＿＿＿＿ ＿＿＿＿＿ a professional.

(2) (a) It's half the size of Kyushu Island.

    (b) It's ＿＿＿＿＿ ＿＿＿＿＿ ＿＿＿＿＿ ＿＿＿＿＿ Kyushu Island.

(3) (a) The sumo wrestler weighs three times my weight.

    (b) I am ＿＿＿＿＿ ＿＿＿＿＿ ＿＿＿＿＿ ＿＿＿＿＿ as the sumo wrestler.

(4) (a) I'm in charge of not only leading a team but also training new employees.

    (b) I'm in charge of training new employees ＿＿＿＿＿ ＿＿＿＿＿ ＿＿＿＿＿

    leading a team.

(5) (a) Please let me know the result as soon as possible.

    (b) Please let me know the result as soon as ＿＿＿＿＿ ＿＿＿＿＿.

(6) (a) I want your explanation rather than your apology.

    (b) I want ＿＿＿＿＿ ＿＿＿＿＿ ＿＿＿＿＿ your apology ＿＿＿＿＿ your

    explanation.

2 例にならって下線部の誤りを訂正し，文全体を書き直しましょう。

(例) My father always <u>keep my</u> promise. → My father always keeps his promise.

(1) The musician has <u>fans as many as</u> Steve. （語順をかえる）

＿＿＿＿＿＿＿＿＿＿＿＿＿＿＿＿＿＿＿＿＿＿＿＿＿＿＿＿＿＿＿＿＿＿

(2) I should have studied as <u>hardly</u> as he did.

＿＿＿＿＿＿＿＿＿＿＿＿＿＿＿＿＿＿＿＿＿＿＿＿＿＿＿＿＿＿＿＿＿＿

(3) The cost of living in this country is many times as <u>highly</u> as that in my home country.

＿＿＿＿＿＿＿＿＿＿＿＿＿＿＿＿＿＿＿＿＿＿＿＿＿＿＿＿＿＿＿＿＿＿

(4) We need <u>more a few</u> people to carry these desks. （語順をかえる）

＿＿＿＿＿＿＿＿＿＿＿＿＿＿＿＿＿＿＿＿＿＿＿＿＿＿＿＿＿＿＿＿＿＿

(5) I walked as <u>long</u> as Tokyo Station.

＿＿＿＿＿＿＿＿＿＿＿＿＿＿＿＿＿＿＿＿＿＿＿＿＿＿＿＿＿＿＿＿＿＿

(6) The number of customers was <u>one half</u> times as large as that of the previous year.

＿＿＿＿＿＿＿＿＿＿＿＿＿＿＿＿＿＿＿＿＿＿＿＿＿＿＿＿＿＿＿＿＿＿

3 日本語の意味に合うように，空所に適切な語を入れましょう。

(1) こんな苦いコーヒーは飲めません。

I can't drink coffee _____ _____ _____ this.

(2) 彼は外見ほど若くはありません。

He isn't _____ _____ _____ he _____.

(3) この川でそこはここより3倍深い。

That point of this river is _____ _____ _____ _____
_____ this point.

(4) 早ければ来月はじめにも私たちは新たなプロジェクトに着手します。

We will start a new project _____ _____ _____ the beginning of
next month.

(5) 彼女は相変わらず人気のある俳優です。

She is _____ popular an actor _____ _____.

(6) その種の哺乳類は高等動物に分類されます。

That kind of mammal is classified as a _____ _____.

4 日本語の意味に合うように，（　　　）内の語句を並べかえましょう。

(1) その仕事は終わったも同然だ。

The task (as / is / as / good / finished).

_____

(2) その新人はベテランスタッフに負けず劣らず仕事が速い。

The newcomer (to / quick / as / work / is / as) the experienced staff members.

_____

(3) 彼はそんなミスをするほど愚かではありません。

He isn't (stupid / make / to / as / so) such a mistake.

_____

(4) 彼女は分別がある点では私のクラスのどの女子にも劣っていません。

She is (any / as / a girl / as / sensible) in my class.

_____

(5) 彼は極めて無礼な人です。　He is (rude / ever / a person / as / lived / as).

_____

(6) 私に関する限り，その問題は簡単に解決できます。

(concerned / I'm / far / as / as), the problem is easy to solve.

_____

43

LESSON 7

比較② （同等比較，倍数比較など）

教科書 pp.50-55

STEP 3 まとめ問題

1 （　　）内の指示にしたがって，与えられた語を必要なら形を変えて使い，英文を完成させましょう。

(1) その辞書ほど役に立つ辞書はありません。(as 〜 as を使って)

_____

(2) 彼女のようにゆっくり話してくれませんか。(slowly, as 〜 as を使って)

_____

(3) 私の知る限りでは，彼女はまだ大学生です。(far)

_____

2 日本語の意味に合うように，英文を完成させましょう。

(1) あなたが必要なだけ箱を持って行ってください。

Take _____.

(2) できるだけ私たちの目的地の近くで会いましょう。

Let's meet at a place that is _____.

(3) 当店では体の大きい男性用のコートも扱っております。

We also have coats _____.

3 次の日本語を英語に直しましょう。

(1) 彼ほど先生に叱られる生徒はいません。

_____

(2) 私たちの赤ちゃんは毎日，私たちの2倍近く長く眠ります。

_____

44

4 次の 4 つの項目を入れて，沙織さんがスマートフォンの普及率について調べた内容の英文を作ってみましょう。

① 日本で現在までにスマートフォンがどれだけ普及しているかに関する情報を，インターネットで探してみた。

② 15 歳から 79 歳まで (aged between 15 and 79) の男女のスマートフォンの保有率に関する調査 (survey) によると，2022 年は 94％で，その率は 10 年前の約 4 倍である。

③ 2022 年の時点で (as of) で 70 歳代は約 (approximately) 70％がスマートフォンを所有している。つまり，まだスマートフォンを持っていない高齢者は多いということである。

④ スマートフォンを持っていない人が持っている人と同様に不自由なく (comfortably) 過ごせる社会にすることが重要だと思う。

_____

_____

_____

_____

_____

🔊 LISTENING

会話を聞いて，(1)〜(4)の内容を書きとりましょう。

エイミーは，先生と投票率について話しています。(*A:* Amy *T:* Teacher)

A: I heard the turnout for the House of Representatives election last week in Japan was about 54%.

T: The turnout in France is below 50%. (1)_____.

A: Really? (2)_____.

T: A survey says that many Japanese people don't think (3)_____ _____ even if they vote in an election.

A: That's too bad.

T: I hope (4)_____.

(1) _____

(2) _____

(3) _____

(4) _____

LESSON 8
動名詞

教科書 pp.58-63

STEP 1 基本問題

① 基本的な動名詞の用法

1 日本語の意味に合うように( )内の語を並べかえ，文全体を書き直しましょう。

(1) 初めての場所を訪れることはわくわくさせます。

(a / place / new / visiting) is exciting.

_____

(2) 私の趣味はパズルを組み立てることです。

My hobby (putting / is / puzzles) together.

_____

(3) 弘は列車の写真を撮ることが好きです。

Hiroshi (likes / pictures / of / taking) trains.

_____

2 次の英文を日本語に訳しましょう。

I'm interested in teaching Japanese to people in other countries.

_____

② 受け身・完了形の動名詞

1 日本語の意味に合うように( )内の語を並べかえ，文全体を書き直しましょう。

(1) 私たちは解雇されるのではないかと心配しました。

We were (fired / about / being / worried).

_____

(2) 彼は自分がそのレースに勝ったことを誇りに思っています。

He is (of / won / proud / having) the race.

_____

2 次の英文を日本語に訳しましょう。

I'm confused about being thought of too highly.

_____

46

❸ 意味上の主語を含む動名詞

1   日本語の意味に合うように(   )内の語を並べかえ，文全体を書き直しましょう。

(1) 窓を開けたままにしておいてもいいですか。

(my / you / would / mind) leaving the window open?

_____

(2) 私は彼が私の事業を引き継ぐと確信しています。

I (am / of / his / sure) taking over my business.

_____

2   次の英文を日本語に訳しましょう。

We objected to him joining our group due to his young age.

_____

❹ 動名詞を用いたさまざまな表現

1   日本語の意味に合うように(   )内の語を並べかえ，文全体を書き直しましょう。

(1) その提案は検討する価値があります。

The proposal (worth / is / considering).

_____

(2) 明日何が起こるのかはわかりません。

(no / there / is / telling) what will happen tomorrow.

_____

(3) 私は食後にいつもコーヒーが飲みたくなります。

I (having / like / feel) a cup of coffee after each meal.

_____

2   次の英文を日本語に訳しましょう。

He will never change his mind. It's no use trying to convince him.

_____

LESSON 8

動名詞

教科書 pp.58-63

STEP 2 実践問題

1 (   )内から適切な語句を選びましょう。

(1) (Live / Living) alone is comfortable for me.

(2) (Keep / Keeping) an eye on a small child.

(3) We enjoyed (to dance / dancing) at the party yesterday.

(4) Stop (to talk / talking) behind people's backs.

(5) Do you remember (to post / posting) her a letter last month?

(6) How about (try / trying) that new Thai restaurant?

(7) He is ashamed of (saying / having said) such a thing at that time.

(8) I hate (called / being called) "Dr." by people around me.

(9) I'm getting used to (work / working) in a new environment.

(10) What do you (tell / say) to going out for dinner tonight?

2 例にならって下線部の誤りを訂正し，文全体を書き直しましょう。

（例）My father always <u>keep my</u> promise. → My father always keeps his promise.

(1) <u>Look</u> at the picture makes me happy.

_____

(2) <u>Being</u> kind to everyone whoever she or he is.

_____

(3) I stopped <u>taking</u> a deep breath because I came in a hurry.

_____

(4) I hope <u>seeing</u> her again in the near future.

_____

(5) I will never forget <u>to visit</u> Egypt last summer.

_____

(6) <u>Making</u> the event a success together is a good memory.

_____

(7) This card is used to <u>unlocking</u> the door of the laboratory.

_____

(8) Please excuse me for <u>late</u>.

_____

48

3 日本語の意味に合うように，空所に適切な語を入れましょう。

(1) 何かを始めることと，それを続けることはどちらが難しいですか。

Which is more difficult, _____ something or _____ it?

(2) その機械の修理はもう終わりましたか。

Have you _____ _____ the machine yet?

(3) 彼は彼女のバッグを盗んでいないと言いました。

He _____ _____ _____ her bag.

(4) 私はいつも朝食を食べる前にジョギングします。

I usually go for a jog _____ _____ breakfast.

(5) 健は自分の申し出が拒絶されることを心配しています。

Ken is afraid of _____ _____ _____ rejected.

(6) その機械の操作ということになると，彼女の右に出る人はいません。

_____ _____ _____ _____ operating the machine, no one is better than her.

4 日本語の意味に合うように，（　　）内の語句を並べかえましょう。

(1) 彼女の趣味は花を栽培することと風景画を描くことです。

Her hobbies (and / growing / drawing / flowers / landscapes / are).

_____

(2) 発表の練習を何度もしておけばよかった。

I (have / practiced / the presentation / should / making) many times.

_____

(3) 彼はお金を使い果たしてしまったと白状しました。

He (out / having / of / to / run / admitted) money.

_____

(4) 発注する前に注文内容を確認してください。

Confirm (to / placing / prior / an order / your purchase).

_____

(5) 私はだれかが困っているのを見ると，何かをせずにはいられません。

I (when / doing / cannot / something / help) I see someone in trouble.

_____

(6) 最終決断に至るとすぐに，私たちはそのプロジェクトを実行に移しました。

(decision / on / at / a final / arriving), we put the project into action.

_____

49

LESSON 8
動名詞
STEP 3 まとめ問題

教科書 pp.58-63

1 ( )内に与えられた語句を必要なら形を変えて使い，英文を完成させましょう。

(1) 脚本を書くことは私にとってとても興味深いです。(write a play)
_____

(2) 私たちは新入社員を迎えることを心待ちにしています。(welcome the new employees)
_____

(3) 今さらそれを後悔しても仕方ありません。(point / regret)
_____

2 日本語の意味に合うように，英文を完成させましょう。

(1) 私たちに歌舞伎を鑑賞するすばらしい機会を与えてくださり，ありがとうございます。
_____ to watch Kabuki.

(2) 彼は人付き合いが得意です。
He _____ along with people.

(3) 私たちはもうすぐ行われる学園祭の準備で忙しい。
_____ the upcoming school festival.

3 次の日本語を英語に直しましょう。

(1) 私は彼が私を避けていることに気づいていました。
_____

(2) 彼女は私にさよならも言わずに去りました。
_____

4 次の4つの項目を入れて，浩二さんが感銘を受けた本の紹介の英文を作ってみましょう。

① この本は医師であった中村哲氏によって書かれた。
② その本は彼が病院で働くためにパキスタンに行ったあとの彼や彼の周りの人々が行ったことについて語っている。
③ 中村医師はパキスタンで人々が飢饉(famine)に苦しむのを見て，まず生活(livelihoods)を支援するために井戸を掘り始めた。さらに，より確実な水の供給のために用水路(irrigation canals)の建設に献身した。
④ 私は彼が人々の幸せのために，たとえそれがどこの(no matter where)人であろうと，長年懸命に働いたことを，1人の日本人として誇りに思います。

___

LISTENING

会話を聞いて，(1)～(4)の内容を書きとりましょう。

ロンは，エイミーおすすめの本を読み終わったようです。(*R:* Ron *A:* Amy)

R: (1)_____. I was moved by Malala's speech.
A: It's my pleasure. Her famous phrase "One pen can change the world" is really impressive.
R: I totally agree with her idea. I think (2)_____.
A: Exactly. I was shocked that Malala was attacked by gunmen who were against her idea.
R: So was I. She received the Nobel Peace Prize (3)_____.
A: Yes. (4)_____.

(1) _____
(2) _____
(3) _____
(4) _____

LESSON 9
to 不定詞

教科書 pp.66-71

STEP 1 基本問題

❶ 名詞的用法

1 日本語の意味に合うように(　)内の語を並べかえ，文全体を書き直しましょう。

(1) 英語の勉強は楽しいです。

　(is / study / English / to) enjoyable.

(2) 私の夢は世界中の人々のために働くことです。

　My dream (for / to / is / work) people all over the world.

(3) 将来，宇宙に行ってみたいですか。

　Do you (to / want / travel) into space in the future?

2 次の英文を日本語に訳しましょう。

　It's not so easy to translate the long English letter into Japanese.

❷ 形容詞的用法

1 日本語の意味に合うように(　)内の語を並べかえ，文全体を書き直しましょう。

(1) 京都は訪れるべきところがたくさんあります。

　Kyoto has (visit / many / to / places).

(2) 何か飲み物をください。

　Please give (to / me / something / drink).

2 次の英文を日本語に訳しましょう。

　I didn't have enough time to check all my answers on the exam.

❸ 副詞的用法

1　日本語の意味に合うように（　　　）内の語句を並べかえ，文全体を書き直しましょう。

(1) 私は本を借りるために図書館に行きました。

I went to the library (to / a book / borrow).

_____

(2) 目が覚めると，家にだれもいないことに気づきました。

I (that / find / awoke / to) no one was at home.

_____

2　次の英文を日本語に訳しましょう。

I'm glad to hear that she's recovering from her disease.

_____

❹ 原形不定詞

1　日本語の意味に合うように（　　　）内の語を並べかえ，文全体を書き直しましょう。

(1) 彼に私の PC を見てもらいたいです。

I want to (at / him / look / have) my PC.

_____

(2) 彼のジョークに私たちは笑いました。

His jokes (laugh / us / made).

_____

(3) 私は遠くでだれかが私の名前を呼ぶのが聞こえました。

I (someone / call / heard) my name in the distance.

_____

2　次の英文を日本語に訳しましょう。

Shall I help you move the piano?

_____

LESSON 9
to 不定詞

教科書 pp.66-71

STEP 2 実践問題

1 (　)内から適切な語句を選びましょう。

(1) I want (something to drink cold / something cold to drink).
(2) Do you still (want / want to) these old magazines?
(3) Let's think about a way (to / is to) solve the problem.
(4) I'm looking forward to (see / seeing) you soon.
(5) Don't forget (to attend / attending) today's meeting, which will start at two.
(6) I told him (keep / to keep) going straight to the next intersection.
(7) Do you know (how changes / how to change) a tire on a car?
(8) Wear a mask (not in order to / in order not to) catch a cold.
(9) We were made (follow / to follow) her instructions.
(10) Let me (make / to make) my own decisions about my future.

2 例にならって下線部の誤りを訂正し，文全体を書き直しましょう。

(例) My father always keep my promise. → My father always keeps his promise.

(1) It is impossible finish reading the report in one day.
_____

(2) We found difficult get used to a new environment.
_____

(3) I was sad hear that she would be leaving our office.
_____

(4) Remember thanking them for their cooperation.
_____

(5) I want to you train new staff members for me today.
_____

(6) I tried to get him change his behavior.
_____

(7) He spent two hours to repair his bike.
_____

(8) How long does it take getting to the hospital by bus?
_____

3 日本語の意味に合うように，空所に適切な語を入れましょう。

(1) 私には新車を買う余裕はありません。

I _____ _____ _____ buy a new car.

(2) 何か言いたいことはありますか。

Do you have _____ _____ _____?

(3) ぐずぐずしている時間はありませんよ。

There is _____ _____ _____ _____.

(4) 実を言うと，彼にはまだそのことについて話していません。

_____ _____ _____ _____, I haven't told him about that yet.

(5) 彼女は突然姿を消して，二度と戻ってきませんでした。

She disappeared suddenly, _____ _____ come back again.

(6) 私はその件と関係がありません。

I _____ _____ _____ _____ _____ the matter.

4 日本語の意味に合うように，（　　　）内の語句を並べかえましょう。

(1) 彼はメジャーリーグでプレーした最初の日本人野球選手でした。

He was (in / Japanese baseball player / play / to / the first) the major leagues.

_____

(2) あなたをこんなに長い時間待たせて，すまないと思います。

I (you / sorry / waiting / to / am / keep) so long.

_____

(3) 彼はパイロットになることを強く望んでいます。

He (a / has / to / desire / great) become a pilot.

_____

(4) 私は新たな経験をするために海外に行きます。

I'm (to / experiences / abroad / new / going / have).

_____

(5) 彼はなぜ大学に進学することを決心したのですか。

(made / decide / him / what / to) go to university?

_____

(6) あなたはそこに行きさえすればよい。

(you / is / all / to / have / do) to go there.

_____

LESSON 9
to 不定詞
教科書 pp.66-71

STEP 3 まとめ問題

1 ( )内に与えられた語句を必要なら形を変えて使い，英文を完成させましょう。

(1) そのアイデアを最初に思いついた人はだれだったのですか。(come up with)
_____

(2) 私はあなたが無事だとわかって安心しています。(relieve / safe)
_____

(3) 私の息子は自分のことは自分でできる年齢です。(enough / take care of)
_____

2 日本語の意味に合うように，英文を完成させましょう。

(1) この授業の目標はあなた方に実用的な英語のスキルを身につけさせることです。
_____ develop practical English skills.

(2) 私は新たな国に事業を拡大する計画について聞きました。
_____ expand our business into a new country.

(3) 彼女と私の見解は違うように思えます。
Her thoughts _____ mine.

3 次の日本語を英語に直しましょう。

(1) 私はスマートフォンでお金を払うのは便利だと思いました。
_____

(2) 私は会社にとどまるように頼まれました。
_____

4 次の4つの項目を入れて，みんなでできる遊びを紹介する英文を作ってみましょう。

① みんなですぐに楽しめるゲームを2つ紹介したい。皆さんはテレビやインターネットでそれらを見たことがあるかもしれない。そのゲームのためにお金を払う必要も，特別な道具(devices)を準備する必要もない。

② 1つは「英語禁止(No English)」ゲーム。ゲーム中は英単語を使ってはならない。あなたは英単語を使うことなく話をすることは難しいと思うかもしれない。

③ もう1つは「おしぼりルーレット(Wet Towel Roulette)」ゲーム。プレーヤーは順番にタオルを絞り(wring)，1滴も水を出せない(cannot squeeze a drop of water out of it)人が負け(loser)だ。

④ テレビゲーム以外のゲームも試してみてはどうだろうか。

_____
_____
_____
_____

LISTENING

会話を聞いて，(1)～(4)の内容を書きとりましょう。

拓は，車いすバスケットボールについてエイミーに話しています。(*T*: Taku *A*: Amy)

T: Yesterday, I watched a wheelchair basketball game in the gym for the first time. I was surprised that (1)_____.

A: Really? There are many kinds of parasports, right?

T: That's right. Players can enjoy sports even though they have disabilities.

A: Each player has a different kind of disability. (2)_____?

T: (3)_____, they can enjoy playing the same sports fairly.

A: That's great! (4)_____.

(1) _____
(2) _____
(3) _____
(4) _____

LESSON 10

分詞

教科書 pp.74-79

STEP 1 基本問題

❶ 現在分詞

1 日本語の意味に合うように（　　　）内の語句を並べかえ，文全体を書き直しましょう。

(1) その眠っている赤ん坊はかわいいです。

(sleeping / the / is / baby) lovely.

_____

(2) 向こうで走っている馬はだれのものですか。

Whose is (over / there / running / the horse)?

_____

2 次の英文を日本語に訳しましょう。

Can you see the man sitting in the front row?

_____

❷ 過去分詞

1 日本語の意味に合うように（　　　）内の語句を並べかえ，文全体を書き直しましょう。

(1) そのビルにはこわれた窓がいくつかあります。

There are (broken / windows / some) in the building.

_____

(2) 彼が撮った写真を見せてください。

Please show me (by / the pictures / him / taken).

_____

2 次の英文を日本語に訳しましょう。

I wonder where the package received by Karen is.

_____

58

❸ 目的語の補語になる分詞

1 日本語の意味に合うように（　　　）内の語句を並べかえ，文全体を書き直しましょう。

(1) 私はティムが駅周辺を歩いているのを見ました。

I (Tim / around / saw / walking) the station.

_____

(2) あなたの名前が呼ばれたのが聞こえましたか。

Did you (hear / name / your / called)?

_____

(3) 機械をしばらく運転し続けておいてください。

(running / keep / the machine) for a while.

_____

2 次の英文を日本語に訳しましょう。

I must get my driver's license renewed.

_____

❹ 分詞を用いたさまざまな表現

1 日本語の意味に合うように（　　　）内の語句を並べかえ，文全体を書き直しましょう。

(1) 友人と話しているとき，友人に何か心配事があるのに気づきました。

(with / my friend / talking), I noticed that he was worried about something.

_____

(2) 遠くから見ると，彼は若く見えました。

(distance / from / seen / a), he looked younger.

_____

(3) 私の経験から判断すると，彼女は才能を活かしきれていません。

(my / from / experience / judging), she hasn't been able to use all her talent.

_____

2 次の英文を日本語に訳しましょう。

The students listened to me with their eyes shining.

_____

59

LESSON 10

分詞

教科書 pp.74-79

STEP 2 実践問題

1 ( )内から適切な語句を選びましょう。

(1) Who is (the talking man / the man talking) to Emily?

(2) My (bag stolen / stolen bag) was found by the police.

(3) She is the author of a novel widely (reading / read) around the world.

(4) There are many people (visiting / visited) Hokkaido.

(5) Watch out for stones (falling / fallen) from the cliff.

(6) I called an ambulance for the (injuring / injured) man.

(7) The shop buys and sells only (using / used) goods.

(8) The noise kept me (irritating / irritated).

(9) She sat on the chair with her arms (folding / folded).

(10) (Writing / Written) in plain English, the book is also popular in Japan.

2 例にならって下線部の誤りを訂正し，文全体を書き直しましょう。

（例）My father always keep my promise. → My father always keeps his promise.

(1) I'm worried about the boy crying.

_____

(2) She has a made car in China.

_____

(3) Our English teacher often tells us interested stories.

_____

(4) Ten people, included Kate and me, are participating in the event.

_____

(5) I went to the dentist to have my tooth fill.

_____

(6) Generally spoken, Japanese people tend not to reveal their intentions.

_____

(7) Tiring of his work, he patiently continued it.

_____

(8) Having not met with him for many years, I didn't recognize him immediately.

_____

3 日本語の意味に合うように，空所に適切な語を入れましょう。

(1) 列の最後に立っている男性があなたのお兄さんですか。

Is the ＿＿＿＿＿＿ ＿＿＿＿＿＿ at the end of the line your brother?

(2) 関心のある生徒は私に連絡するように。

＿＿＿＿＿＿ ＿＿＿＿＿＿ must contact me.

(3) 彼はその店で高価な腕時計を購入しているところを見られました。

He ＿＿＿＿＿＿ ＿＿＿＿＿＿ ＿＿＿＿＿＿ an expensive watch at the shop.

(4) 彼は彼女の親切に感謝しながら，去って行きました。

He left, ＿＿＿＿＿＿ her ＿＿＿＿＿＿ her kindness.

(5) 天気がよければ，渓流釣りに行きたい。

＿＿＿＿＿＿ ＿＿＿＿＿＿, I want to go fishing in a mountain stream.

(6) 彼の努力を考慮に入れて，もう1度チャンスを与えましょう。

＿＿＿＿＿＿ his efforts ＿＿＿＿＿＿ ＿＿＿＿＿＿, I will give him another chance.

4 日本語の意味に合うように，（　　）内の語句を並べかえましょう。

(1) マスクをして車の修理をしている人が高橋さんです。

(a car / a mask / the man / and / wearing / repairing) is Mr. Takahashi.

＿＿＿＿＿＿＿＿＿＿＿＿＿＿＿＿＿＿＿＿＿＿＿＿＿＿＿＿＿＿＿＿＿＿

(2) その場所は落ち葉に覆われていました。

The area (leaves / with / covered / fallen / was).

＿＿＿＿＿＿＿＿＿＿＿＿＿＿＿＿＿＿＿＿＿＿＿＿＿＿＿＿＿＿＿＿＿＿

(3) 彼はその知らせに興奮するあまり，なかなか眠れませんでした。

He (excited / the news / so / that / was / by) he had difficulty sleeping.

＿＿＿＿＿＿＿＿＿＿＿＿＿＿＿＿＿＿＿＿＿＿＿＿＿＿＿＿＿＿＿＿＿＿

(4) 私たちの計画を受け入れてもらうためには何をすればいいのだろうか。

What should we do (to / our / accepted / have / plans)?

＿＿＿＿＿＿＿＿＿＿＿＿＿＿＿＿＿＿＿＿＿＿＿＿＿＿＿＿＿＿＿＿＿＿

(5) どうしていいかわからなかったので，私は彼女に助言を求めました。

(to / knowing / what / do / not), I asked her for some advice.

＿＿＿＿＿＿＿＿＿＿＿＿＿＿＿＿＿＿＿＿＿＿＿＿＿＿＿＿＿＿＿＿＿＿

(6) 小さな子どもを水辺で遊ばせておかないように。

(never / small / playing / children / leave) near water.

＿＿＿＿＿＿＿＿＿＿＿＿＿＿＿＿＿＿＿＿＿＿＿＿＿＿＿＿＿＿＿＿＿＿

LESSON 10
分詞

教科書 pp.74-79

STEP 3 まとめ問題

1 (　　)内に与えられた語句を必要なら形を変えて使い，英文を完成させましょう。

(1) プレゼンテーションをしている女性は医師です。(give a presentation)

_____

(2) 私たちに混乱させるような情報を与えないでください。(confuse)

_____

(3) 彼女は髪を風になびかせて走っていました。(with / blow)

_____

2 日本語の意味に合うように，英文を完成させましょう。

(1) 彼女が書いた本のタイトルは何ですか。

What is the title of _____?

(2) これは私が今まで見た中でいちばん退屈なテレビドラマです。

_____ I have ever seen.

3 次の英文を指示にしたがって書き直しましょう。

(1) When I was walking in a strange city, I happened upon an acquaintance. （分詞構文で）

_____

(2) Because it started to rain, we took a taxi. （分詞構文で）

_____

(3) Having had a similar experience, I understand your feelings. （接続詞を使って）

_____

62

4 次の4つの項目を入れて，ニュース番組の原稿を英語で作ってみましょう。

① News Today です。今日のニュースをお伝えします(Here is 〜)。

② 皆さんはサルが近くを通り過ぎていく(pass nearby)のを見たことがありますか。最近，市内にサルが現れたというニュースを何度かお伝えしましたが，今日はさかえ町で1匹のサルが目撃されました。

③ 警察が通報(a call)を受けて5時間以上かけて捕獲を試みるも，結局，見失いました(lose sight of)。

④ 幸いサルに襲われ(attack)た人はいませんでしたが，サルを見かけても決して近づかないようにしてください。

LISTENING

会話を聞いて，(1)〜(4)の内容を書きとりましょう。

ニュースを見たエイミーは，あることを心配しています。(*A*: Amy *T*: Taku)

A: Did you hear about the accident in the Indian Ocean?

T: The Indian Ocean? No, I didn't.

A: On TV, (1)_____. Seen from the sky, the Indian Ocean looks almost black. I suppose (2)_____.

T: That's too bad. I can easily imagine how hard it is to solve this problem.

A: (3)_____, sometimes more than a year. Besides, it costs a lot.

T: Unbelievable. All I can do now is to hope (4)_____.

(1) _____
(2) _____
(3) _____
(4) _____

LESSON 11

関係詞① （関係代名詞）

教科書 pp.80-85

STEP 1 基本問題

❶ 基本的な関係代名詞の用法

1 日本語の意味に合うように（　　）内の語句を並べかえ，文全体を書き直しましょう。

(1) 昨日開かれた協議会に参加しましたか。

Did you take part in (held / which / was / the conference) yesterday?

_____

(2) 彼が結婚した女性は弁護士です。

(who / the woman / married / he) is a lawyer.

_____

(3) 必要なものを教えてください。

Tell me (is / what / needed).

_____

2 次の英文を日本語に訳しましょう。

Did you return the book that you borrowed a week ago?

_____

❷ 所有格 whose

1 日本語の意味に合うように（　　）内の語句を並べかえ，文全体を書き直しましょう。

(1) 母親が教師であるその少年も教師を目指しています。

The boy (whose / a teacher / mother / is) also wants to become a teacher.

_____

(2) 屋根が赤い家が私の家です。

The house (is / whose / red / roof) is mine.

_____

2 次の英文を日本語に訳しましょう。

I work for a company whose head office is in the U.S.A.

_____

64

❸ 関係代名詞の非制限用法

1　日本語の意味に合うように（　　）内の語句を並べかえ，文全体を書き直しましょう。

(1) 私たちは皆，彼を信頼しています。決してうそをつかないからです。

All of us trust him, (tells / a lie / who / never).

_____

(2) その家族は海外から越してきたのですが，すぐにここでの生活に慣れました。

The family, (from / who / moved / abroad), got used to living here easily.

_____

(3) こちらは今井さんで，私は自分が小さい頃から知っています。

This is Ms. Imai, (I / known / have / whom) since I was a child.

_____

2　次の英文を日本語に訳しましょう。

One of his works, which was written a few hundred years ago, is still popular.

_____

❹ 複合関係代名詞

1　日本語の意味に合うように（　　）内の語句を並べかえ，文全体を書き直しましょう。

(1) 当クラブに入会したい方はだれでも歓迎します。

We will welcome (wants / join / whoever / to) our club.

_____

(2) ここで生じたことは何でも私に報告すること。

Report (here / occurs / whatever) to me.

_____

(3) だれに責任があるにせよ，私たち皆が解決策を考えるべきです。

(whoever / the responsibility / has), all of us should think of a solution.

_____

2　次の英文を日本語に訳しましょう。

Whichever you choose, there is not much difference.

_____

LESSON 11

関係詞①（関係代名詞）

教科書 pp.80-85

STEP 2 実践問題

1 (   )内から適切な語句を選びましょう。

(1) That's (which / what) you said yesterday.

(2) Are animals (who / that) are in zoos happy?

(3) There are three employees (that / whom) will receive an award.

(4) The apartment house, (which / whose) bathrooms are shared by the residents, will be repaired next month.

(5) He is not (that / what) he was.

(6) Who was the person (to who / to whom) you spoke yesterday?

(7) Today I didn't see the boy and his dog (which / that) run in the park every day.

(8) This is the pen (with which / with that) the novelist wrote his novels.

(9) He said that he could speak English, (that / which) was a lie.

(10) If (whoever / anyone) is having difficulty hearing me, let me know.

2 例にならって下線部の誤りを訂正し，文全体を書き直しましょう。

(例) My father always keep my promise. → My father always keeps his promise.

(1) I want to ask for the opinion of someone which is familiar with the law.

_____

(2) I looked up which I wanted to know in the encyclopedia.

_____

(3) The report mentions something what is important to our lives.

_____

(4) This is the picture which Allen is proud.

_____

(5) I learned the procedure from him, who was a mistake.

_____

(6) He, which father is the president of the company, got promoted.

_____

(7) Whoever win first prize in the contest, it matters little to me.

_____

(8) Which is more, they revealed an unexpected finding.

_____

3 日本語の意味に合うように，空所に適切な語を入れましょう。

(1) 私が欲しいそのカメラは入手困難です。

The camera ＿＿＿＿＿ ＿＿＿＿＿ ＿＿＿＿＿ is difficult to get.

(2) 私は昨日，友人と会いましたが，その友人の兄は私の義理の兄です。

I met a friend of mine yesterday, ＿＿＿＿＿ ＿＿＿＿＿ is my brother-in-law.

(3) 始まりがあるものはすべて終わりがあります。

＿＿＿＿＿ ＿＿＿＿＿ a beginning ＿＿＿＿＿ an end.

(4) 彼女はいわゆる生き字引(歩く辞書)です。

She is ＿＿＿＿＿ ＿＿＿＿＿ ＿＿＿＿＿ "a walking dictionary."

(5) その木は葉が全部落ちてしまいましたが，来年また葉が生い茂るでしょう。

The tree, all the leaves ＿＿＿＿＿ ＿＿＿＿＿ have fallen, will be thick with leaves again next year.

4 日本語の意味に合うように，(　　)内の語句を並べかえましょう。

(1) 京都は私が日本で行ったことがある中で最も美しい場所です。

Kyoto is the most beautiful place (ever / I / to / have / that / been) in Japan.

＿＿＿＿＿＿＿＿＿＿＿＿＿＿＿＿＿＿＿＿＿＿＿＿＿＿＿＿＿＿＿

(2) だれも彼女の才能を評価しませんが，私はすばらしいと思います。

No one appreciates (is / I / great / which / think / her talent,).

＿＿＿＿＿＿＿＿＿＿＿＿＿＿＿＿＿＿＿＿＿＿＿＿＿＿＿＿＿＿＿

(3) 今日の私があるのは周りの人たちのおかげです。

People around me (I / made / what / am / me) today.

＿＿＿＿＿＿＿＿＿＿＿＿＿＿＿＿＿＿＿＿＿＿＿＿＿＿＿＿＿＿＿

(4) 多くの日本人がその意味を知らない日本語はたくさんあります。

There are a lot of Japanese words (many / don't / whose / know / meanings / Japanese people).

＿＿＿＿＿＿＿＿＿＿＿＿＿＿＿＿＿＿＿＿＿＿＿＿＿＿＿＿＿＿＿

(5) あなたがどのような道を選んでも，私たちはあなたを応援します。

(take / course / choose / whatever / to / you), we will support you.

＿＿＿＿＿＿＿＿＿＿＿＿＿＿＿＿＿＿＿＿＿＿＿＿＿＿＿＿＿＿＿

(6) あなたのうちのどちらがその方法を試してみても，結果は同じでしょう。

(of / the method / whichever / you / tries), the result will be the same.

＿＿＿＿＿＿＿＿＿＿＿＿＿＿＿＿＿＿＿＿＿＿＿＿＿＿＿＿＿＿＿

LESSON 11
関係詞① （関係代名詞）

教科書 pp.80-85

STEP 3 まとめ問題

1 （　　）内の指示にしたがって，与えられた語句を必要なら形を変えて使い，英文を完成させましょう。

(1) 私が所属する部署は3階にあります。(section / belong to, 関係代名詞を使って)

_____

(2) 彼は10時広島発の列車に乗り遅れました。(関係代名詞を使って)

_____

2 （　　）内の指示にしたがって，日本語の意味に合うように，英文を完成させましょう。

(1) 彼らは労働環境の改善を約束しましたが，私は不可能だとわかりました。

(関係代名詞を使って)

They promised to improve working conditions, _____.

(2) ヒロシは普段は仕事に遅刻しませんが，今日は遅れて来ました。(関係代名詞を使って)

Hiroshi, _____, arrived late today.

3 （　　）内の指示にしたがって，次の日本語を英語に直しましょう。

(1) だれが私に会いに来ても，私は会うつもりはありません。(複合関係代名詞を使って)

_____

(2) 彼が新しい社長に選ばれましたが,それは私が予想したことでした。(関係代名詞を使って)

_____

4 次の英文を日本語に訳しましょう。

(1) I attended the meeting, during which I dozed off.

_____

(2) Whatever excuse you think of, you won't be able to convince her.

_____

5 次の４つの項目を入れて、職業体験参加を募集する英文を作ってみましょう。

① 幼稚園での職業体験 (work experience program) に参加したい生徒を募集している。
② 参加者 (participants) はグループに分かれて、それぞれ１か所の幼稚園に行く。興味がある人はだれでも参加できるが、定員は 15 名 (参加者は生徒 15 名に制限される)。
③ 用紙に記入し (fill out the form)、遊ぶ、お絵かきをするなど、子どもたちとしてみたいことを書いて提出すること。本を持っていったり、紙芝居 (pictures to tell a story) を準備したりしてもよい。
④ 子どもたちと楽しい時間を過ごしてみませんか。

_____
_____
_____
_____

🔊 LISTENING

次の英文を聞いて、(1)～(4)の内容を書きとりましょう。

華とロンがチョコレートについて話しています。(*H*: Hana *R*: Ron)

H: I found these chocolates at a supermarket.
R: Oh, they're what is called "fair trade" products. (1)_____.
    Compared with regular products, (2)_____.
H: Why is that?
R: (3)_____. So (4)_____.
H: I see. I'll try to choose "fair trade" products when I find them.

(1) _____
(2) _____
(3) _____
(4) _____

LESSON 12
関係詞② （関係副詞）

教科書 pp.88-93

STEP 1 基本問題

❶ 基本的な関係副詞の用法

1　日本語の意味に合うように（　　）内の語句を並べかえ，文全体を書き直しましょう。

(1) 私が生まれた日は大雪でした。

It snowed heavily (the / on / when / day) I was born.

_____

(2) ここは私たちが以前よく野球をした公園です。

This is (we / the park / used to / where) play baseball.

_____

(3) 彼は遅刻した理由を説明しませんでした。

He didn't explain (the reason / he / why / was) late.

_____

2　次の英文を日本語に訳しましょう。

Will you show me how the machine works?

_____

❷ 関係副詞の非制限用法

1　日本語の意味に合うように（　　）内の語句を並べかえ，文全体を書き直しましょう。

(1) 彼らは 7 時に私の家に到着して，それからパーティーが始まりました。

They arrived at my house at seven, (started / the party / when).

_____

(2) 私はパリが好きで，そこに 1 年間住んでいます。

I like Paris, (lived / I / have / where) for a year.

_____

2　次の英文を日本語に訳しましょう。

He stayed in the U.S.A. until last week, when he left for Canada.

_____

70

③ 複合関係副詞

1 日本語の意味に合うように（　　）内の語を並べかえ，文全体を書き直しましょう。

(1) 可能なときはいつでも，私は家で食事をします。

I have a meal at home (it / whenever / possible / is).

_____

(2) 私の息子は私が行くところはどこにでもついて来ます。

My son follows me (I / go / wherever).

_____

2 次の英文を日本語に訳しましょう。

Whenever you find an English word you don't know, look it up in the dictionary.

_____

④ 譲歩を表す複合関係副詞

1 日本語の意味に合うように（　　）内の語句を並べかえ，文全体を書き直しましょう。

(1) どんなに遅くなっても，必ず電話をください。

(late / however / are / you), be sure to call me.

_____

(2) いつチャンスが巡ってきても，私は期待を超える準備ができています。

(arises / an opportunity / whenever), I'm prepared to exceed expectations.

_____

(3) あなたがどこに住んでいても，あなたに幸多からんことを願っています。

(wherever / live / you), I wish you good luck.

_____

2 次の英文を日本語に訳しましょう。

Wherever the plant is grown, it will thrive.

_____

LESSON 12
関係詞② （関係副詞）

教科書 pp.88-93

STEP 2 実践問題

1 例にならって下線部の誤りを訂正し，関係副詞を使って文全体を書き直しましょう。

（例）My father always <u>keep my</u> promise. → My father always keeps his promise.

(1) There was a time <u>which</u> I was good at running.

_____

(2) Linda works at the company <u>at where</u> I worked before.

_____

(3) I have no idea <u>which</u> he wants to quit his job.

_____

(4) <u>On every place</u> she appears, many people gather around her.

_____

(5) This book includes <u>how</u> make good coffee.

_____

2 次の英語を関係副詞を使った文に直しましょう。

(1) You should be careful of the timing at which you tell the truth.

_____

(2) I want to go to the place at which people can relax.

_____

(3) I want to see the way in which she shows her leadership.

_____

(4) That is the reason for which he recovered so soon.

_____

(5) We climbed to the top of a mountain, and we camped there.

_____

(6) Come tomorrow, and then I will have more time.

_____

(7) I will take you to any place you want to visit.

_____

(8) Every time I come here, I see someone I know.

_____

3 日本語の意味に合うように，空所に適切な語を入れましょう。

(1) コンピュータスキルを活かすことができる仕事を探しています。

I'm looking for a _____ _____ I can make use of my computer skills.

(2) 朝は日光を浴びるべき時間です。

_____ _____ _____ we should soak up the sun.

(3) ビルはよく口に食べ物を含んだまましゃべります。だから嫌いなのです。

Bill often talks with his mouth full. _____ _____ _____ I don't

like him.

(4) このようにして研究者としての私のキャリアが始まりました。

_____ _____ _____ my career as a researcher started.

(5) どこでも好きなところに座っていいですよ。

You can sit _____ _____ like.

(6) それがどんなに大変でも，私はその仕事をやり遂げます。

I will complete the task, _____ _____ it is.

4 日本語の意味に合うように，(　　)内の語句を並べかえましょう。

(1) あなたがそのことを後悔する日が来るでしょう。

The day will (it / will / come / you / regret / when).

_____

(2) 努力が報われない場合もあります。

There are (rewarded / cases / our efforts / where / aren't).

_____

(3) 私が勉強が好きな理由は特にありません。

(reason / is / no / why / particular / there) I like studying.

_____

(4) 上司は怒ったお客様にどのように対処すべきか私たちに教えました。

Our boss told us (should / with / we / how / deal) angry customers.

_____

(5) 彼は乗り物に乗るといつも気分が悪くなります。

He gets sick (vehicles / rides / whenever / in / he).

_____

(6) どのように考えても，それは大問題です。

(look / it / however / at / you), it's a big problem.

_____

LESSON 12
関係詞② （関係副詞）

教科書 pp.88-93

STEP 3 まとめ問題

1 （　　）内に与えられた語句を必要なら形を変えて使い，関係副詞を使って英文を完成させましょう。

(1) 私が 7 時に出かけようとしたちょうどその時に電話がありました。(get a call)

_____

(2) ここが自動車事故が起こった場所です。(car accident)

_____

2 日本語の意味に合うように，関係副詞を使って英文を完成させましょう。

(1) 私たちが座っているところからステージの隅は見えません。

We can't see the corner of the stage _____.

(2) それらの動物たちが食べ物を得る方法は興味深い。

_____ is interesting.

3 次の日本語を英語に直しましょう。

(1) 私は初めてあなたと会ったときのことを決して忘れません。

_____

(2) 夢を実現することがどんなに難しくても，簡単に諦めるべきではありません。

_____

4 次の英文を日本語に訳しましょう。

(1) Why she didn't come to the party is because she had a schedule conflict.

_____

(2) Wherever I go, I always pay attention to my surroundings.

_____

5 次の４つの項目を入れて，訪れてみたい国についての英文を作ってみましょう。

① なぜ良い観光地(tourist site)としてスイスを薦めるのかを話します。

② スイスと言えば，日本の人気アニメ(animation series)で見られる美しい風景を思い出すかもしれないが，実際のスイスの風景はもっとずっと雄大(grand)で美しい。

③ スイスにはチューリッヒ(Zurich)のように可愛らしい(lovely)街があり，そこでは居心地の良さを感じることができる。

④ 比較的治安が良く，交通の便が良い(has a good public transportation system)ので，観光客が旅を楽しむのにすばらしい国である。

_____

_____

_____

_____

_____

🔊 LISTENING

会話を聞いて，(1)〜(4)の内容を書きとりましょう。

華とロンは学校に行けない子どもについて話しています。(*H:* Hana　*R:* Ron)

H: Many children cannot go to school (1)_____,
because they have to work for their families.

R: (2)_____ even if they want to.

H: Me neither. I think (3)_____.

R: I quite agree with you, Hana.

H: What should we do to solve this problem?

R: First of all, (4)_____. The more people know
about it, the more ideas will come out.

(1) _____

(2) _____

(3) _____

(4) _____

75

LESSON 13

仮定法

教科書 pp.94-99

STEP 1 基本問題

① 仮定法過去

1　日本語の意味に合うように(　　)内の語を並べかえ，文全体を書き直しましょう。

(1) 彼はもっと懸命に練習すれば，強い選手になれるだろうに。

(harder / he / if / practiced), he could be a strong player.

_____

(2) 私があなたなら，その申し出を受け入れるだろう。

(were / if / you / I), I would accept the offer.

_____

2　次の英文を日本語に訳しましょう。

If someone knew his contact information, we could notify him.

_____

② 仮定法過去完了

1　日本語の意味に合うように(　　)内の語を並べかえ，文全体を書き直しましょう。

(1) もしあなたがその時そこにいたならば，そのパフォーマンスを見ることができただろうに。

(had / you / been / if) there at that time, you could have seen the performance.

_____

(2) もう少し早く家を出ていたら，その電車に間に合っていたかもしれません。

If I had left home a little earlier, (might / I / been / have) on time for the train.

_____

2　次の英文を日本語に訳しましょう。

If he had explained the process in detail, we could have given him more support.

_____

❸ if 節を使わない仮定法

1　日本語の意味に合うように（　　）内の語を並べかえ，文全体を書き直しましょう。

(1) 彼らの協力がなければ，その試みは成功しないだろう。

The attempt wouldn't be successful (collaboration / their / without).

(2) 私はすぐに出発しました。そうでなければ，遅刻していたでしょう。

I started at once, (I / have / otherwise / would) been late.

(3) もっと時間があれば，問題をすべて解くことができたのに。

I could have answered all the questions (with / time / more).

2　次の英文を日本語に訳しましょう。

The doctor that was featured on TV would be able to cure your disease.

❹ 仮定法のさまざまな表現

1　日本語の意味に合うように（　　）内の語を並べかえ，文全体を書き直しましょう。

(1) 学校でテストがなければ，私は決して勉強しないだろう。

(were / if / it / not) for tests at school, I would never study.

(2) あなたがいなかったら，だれも何をすればいいかわからなかっただろう。

If (had / been / not / it) for you, no one would have known what to do.

(3) あなたはもう決断してもいい頃です。

It's (made / time / high / you) a decision.

2　次の英文を日本語に訳しましょう。

It's about time you took your medicine.

77

LESSON 13

仮定法

教科書 pp.94-99

STEP 2 実践問題

1 （　　）内から適切な語句を選びましょう。

(1) If I (learn / learned) to use a PC, I could easily find a job.

(2) If I (am / were) in your position, I would be against the plan.

(3) If you (were / had been) awake at that time, you would have noticed someone coming in.

(4) I studied hard, (and / otherwise) I would have failed the exam.

(5) If he had not lied to us two years ago, we (would trust / would have trusted) him now.

(6) If (it wouldn't be for / it were not for) hope, we would make no effort.

(7) I declined your offer yesterday, but I wish I (have eaten / had eaten) out with you.

2 （　　）内の指示にしたがって，文全体を書き直しましょう。

(1) I don't have enough money to buy the new type of smartphone I want.

（仮定法を使って）

_____

(2) Since you followed the doctor's advice, you are healthy now.　（仮定法を使って）

_____

(3) Without an alarm clock, I would be late for school every day.

（下線部を if を使った文に）

_____

(4) If there had not been the funding, we could not have carried out the project.

（下線部を it を使った文に）

_____

(5) If she were to resign as chairperson, who on earth could take over her position?

（下線部を 1 語で）

_____

(6) I'm sorry I cannot afford to pay for you.　（仮定法の表現を使って）

_____

(7) I don't like to be treated like a child.　（仮定法の表現を使って）

_____

78

3 日本語の意味に合うように，空所に適切な語を入れましょう。

(1) 頼まれれば，私が行くのに。

I would go if I ＿＿＿＿＿＿＿ ＿＿＿＿＿＿＿.

(2) あなたの適切な判断がなかったら，私たちはその危機を乗り越えることができなかったでしょう。

＿＿＿＿＿＿＿ ＿＿＿＿＿＿＿ ＿＿＿＿＿＿＿ ＿＿＿＿＿＿＿ for your proper judgement, we could not have overcome the crisis.

(3) その家族と一緒にいた間，もっと思い出を作っていたらなあ。

I ＿＿＿＿＿＿＿ I ＿＿＿＿＿＿＿ ＿＿＿＿＿＿＿ more memories while I was staying with the family.

(4) 水がなければ，何も生き残ることはできません。

＿＿＿＿＿＿＿ ＿＿＿＿＿＿＿ water, nothing could survive.

(5) 私がもう少し若ければ，登山を続けるだろうに。

＿＿＿＿＿＿＿ ＿＿＿＿＿＿＿ a little younger, I would continue climbing mountains.

4 日本語の意味に合うように，（　　）内の語句を並べかえましょう。

(1) もしあなたが市長に選ばれたら，町をどう変えたいですか。

If you were elected mayor, (want / change / you / how / to / would) the city?

＿＿＿＿＿＿＿＿＿＿＿＿＿＿＿＿＿＿＿＿＿＿＿＿＿＿＿＿＿＿＿＿＿＿＿＿

(2) 私にもっと経験があったならば，その問題をもっとうまく処理できたのに。

If (had / experience / had / more / I), I could have handled the problem better.

＿＿＿＿＿＿＿＿＿＿＿＿＿＿＿＿＿＿＿＿＿＿＿＿＿＿＿＿＿＿＿＿＿＿＿＿

(3) 私にもっと才能があればなあ。

(were / if / I / only / more) talented.

＿＿＿＿＿＿＿＿＿＿＿＿＿＿＿＿＿＿＿＿＿＿＿＿＿＿＿＿＿＿＿＿＿＿＿＿

(4) 質問がございましたら，遠慮なくお電話ください。

(questions / you / any / should / have), please don't hesitate to call us.

＿＿＿＿＿＿＿＿＿＿＿＿＿＿＿＿＿＿＿＿＿＿＿＿＿＿＿＿＿＿＿＿＿＿＿＿

(5) 彼女は幽霊を見たかのように驚いた表情をしていました。

She looked (if / seen / she / as / surprised / had) a ghost.

＿＿＿＿＿＿＿＿＿＿＿＿＿＿＿＿＿＿＿＿＿＿＿＿＿＿＿＿＿＿＿＿＿＿＿＿

(6) あなたが入院していたことを知っていたら，お見舞いに行ったのに。

(the hospital / known / in / you / had / I / were), I would have come to see you.

＿＿＿＿＿＿＿＿＿＿＿＿＿＿＿＿＿＿＿＿＿＿＿＿＿＿＿＿＿＿＿＿＿＿＿＿

LESSON 13
仮定法

教科書 pp.94-99

STEP 3 まとめ問題

1 ( )内に与えられた語句を必要なら形を変えて使い，英文を完成させましょう。

(1) あなたが人前で話すのが得意であれば，私の代わりをしてもらいたいのだが。

(speak in public / take my place)

_____

(2) 彼はその題目について何も知らなかったのに，あたかも専門家のように話しました。

(subject / expert)

_____

2 日本語の意味に合うように，英文を完成させましょう。

(1) 彼女のゴールがなかったら，私たちはそのサッカーの試合に負けただろう。

_____ her goal, we would have lost the soccer game.

(2) 彼はまるで他のだれかに起きたことであるかのように，そのことに無関心でした。

He was indifferent to the matter _____.

3 次の日本語を英語に直しましょう。

(1) 昨日雨がひどく降らなかったら，今日私たちは野球場を使えるのに。

_____

(2) 私は彼にもっとやさしくしていればよかった。

_____

4 次の英文を日本語に訳しましょう。

(1) Twenty years ago, no one would have believed such a thing.

_____

(2) Born in the time when there were no smartphones, we would have suffered inconvenience.

_____

80

5 次の 4 つの項目を入れて，世界の問題についての英文を作ってみましょう。

① 世界では 10 秒に 1 人の子どもが飢餓で亡くなっている。戦争や地域紛争（regional conflicts）が弱い（vulnerable）子どもたちに多大な影響を与えている。

② 一方，日本では毎年 600 万トン以上の食料が廃棄（dispose of）されている。

③ あなたはそれを問題視して（take it seriously）いないかもしれないが，もしお腹をすかせた子どもたちが目の前にいたら，あなたはまだ食べられる食べ物を捨てる（throw away）だろうか。

④ 食べ物を無駄にする（waste）ことなく，世界中の人々が食べ物を共有すれば［していれば］いいのにと思う。

_____

_____

_____

_____

🔊 LISTENING

会話を聞いて，(1)～(4)の内容を書きとりましょう。

エイミーは，ロボット工学の教授に話を聞いています。（*A:* Amy   *P:* Professor）

A: Wow, there are many robots in this laboratory! This one here is moving very smoothly and talking naturally.

P: You are very interested in robotics, aren't you? (1)_____, AI in short.

A: Robots and AI are helping us a lot in our daily lives.

P: That's true. (2)_____, many companies and factories would be in big trouble.

A: Although AI is very convenient, (3)_____.

P: Indeed. (4)_____.

(1) _____

(2) _____

(3) _____

(4) _____

LESSON 14

特殊構文
教科書 pp.100-105

STEP 1 基本問題

❶ 条件・譲歩を表す場合

1 日本語の意味に合うように（　　）内の語を並べかえ，文全体を書き直しましょう。

(1) 私が遅れる場合は，私抜きで始めてください。

(late / case / in / I'm), start without me.

_____

(2) 私たちはここにいる限り，安全です。

(as / we / as / long) are here, we are safe.

_____

(3) 彼はたとえそのテーマについてほとんど知らなくても，知っているかのように話します。

(even / knows / if / he) little about the subject, he speaks as if he does.

_____

2 次の英文を日本語に訳しましょう。

My brother works to pay my school fees even though he is still a student.

_____

❷ 目的・理由を表す場合

1 日本語の意味に合うように（　　）内の語句を並べかえ，文全体を書き直しましょう。

(1) 彼女の両親は彼女が夢を実現できるように応援しました。

Her parents supported her (that / so / could / she) realize her dream.

_____

(2) 私の父はとても弱っていて，杖なしで歩けませんでした。

My father (so / that / weak / was) he couldn't walk without a stick.

_____

(3) 会社に大いに貢献したことを考慮すると，彼女が昇進すべきです。

(given / has contributed / that / she) greatly to the company, she should get promoted.

_____

2 次の英文を日本語に訳しましょう。

Now that the two groups have reached an agreement, things will be better.

_____

❸ 無生物主語を伴う場合

1 日本語の意味に合うように（　　）内の語句を並べかえ，文全体を書き直しましょう。

(1) 彼は勇気を出して新しいビジネスを始めました。

(him / his courage / enabled / to) start a new business.

_____

(2) 彼女は風邪のため，登校できませんでした。

(her cold / her / prevented / from) going to school.

_____

(3) なぜあなたは約束を破ったのですか。

(made / break / you / what) your promise?

_____

2 次の英文を日本語に訳しましょう。

Modern communication technology enables us to work from home more easily.

_____

❹ 強調する場合

1 日本語の意味に合うように（　　）内の語句を並べかえ，文全体を書き直しましょう。

(1) そのドレスはあなたに本当に似合っているわ。

That dress (look / on / does / good) you.

_____

(2) 私が読みたいのはこの本です。

(is / that / this book / it) I want to read.

_____

2 次の英文を日本語に訳しましょう。

All you have to do is to add hot water to eat it.

_____

LESSON 14

特殊構文

教科書 pp.100-105

STEP 2 実践問題

1 ( )内から適切な語句を選びましょう。

(1) As (long / far) as I can work, I will not have trouble making a living.

(2) "Why didn't you go to a hospital yesterday?" "I did (went / go)."

(3) What made you (leave / to leave) the company?

(4) His honesty doesn't allow him (tell / to tell) a lie.

2 例にならって下線部の誤りを訂正し，文全体を書き直しましょう。

(例) My father always keep my promise. → My father always keeps his promise.

(1) In case you will miss the train, please contact me as soon as possible.

_____

(2) Unless you aren't rude to him, he will respond to your request.

_____

(3) We need to use electric devices to some extent, if we like it or not.

_____

(4) He is so a tall man that I asked him to get me the item on the top shelf.

_____

3 ( )内の指示にしたがって，文全体を書き直しましょう。

(1) We should prepare food and water for a few days for an emergency.

（下線部を in case を使った文に）

_____

(2) I got up early in order to submit the report earlier than my classmates.

（下線部が節になるように）

_____

(3) We can only wait for him to come back. （All で始まる文に）

_____

(4) He bought the bike at that shop. （下線部を強調する文に）

_____

(5) He couldn't admit what he did due to his pride. （allow を使った文に）

_____

84

4 日本語の意味に合うように，空所に適切な語を入れましょう。

(1) 私が知る限り，彼に責めはありません。

_____ _____ _____ I know, he is not to blame.

(2) たとえすぐには成功しなくても，努力し続けるべきです。

_____ _____ you don't succeed easily, you should continue to try.

(3) 彼が来ようと来まいと，人は足りています。

_____ he comes _____ _____, we have enough people.

(4) ぜひ来てよ。みんな，あなたに会うのを楽しみにしているから。

Please _____ _____. Everyone is looking forward to seeing you.

(5) あなたが日中に眠いのは，夜更かしするからです。

_____ _____ _____ you stay up late at night that you are sleepy in the day time.

(6) この写真を見ると，私は子どもの頃を思い出します。

This picture _____ me _____ my childhood.

5 日本語の意味に合うように，（　　）内の語を並べかえましょう。ただし，不要な語が１つずつ入っています。

(1) 選手がゲーム中にけがをした場合に備えて，補欠３名がベンチに追加されました。

Three reserves were added to the bench (any / injured / in / players / of / got / case).

_____

(2) 私が生きている限り，そのような邪悪な行為は認めません。

I will not allow such evil conduct (long / will / as / live / I / as).

_____

(3) 彼女は疲れすぎていない限り，毎日夜遅くまで勉強します。

She studies until late at night every day (tired / she / too / unless / if / is).

_____

(4) 重要性にかかわらず，決定は私たちの話し合いによりなされます。

Decisions will be made through our discussion, (are / trivial / important / they / even / or / whether).

_____

(5) それはとてもすばらしい映画だったので，私はみんなにそれを薦めました。

It was (great / such / movie / a / I / very / that) recommended it to everyone.

_____

LESSON 14
特殊構文
STEP 3 まとめ問題

教科書 pp.100-105

1 ( )内に与えられた語句を必要なら形を変えて使い，英文を完成させましょう。

(1) 私たちは彼女の指示にしたがっていればよい。(all / follow instructions)

_____

(2) 責任があるのは彼女ではなく彼です。(it / but)

_____

(3) 駅から徒歩 10 分で博物館に着きました。(bring / me)

_____

2 指示がある場合はそれにしたがい，日本語の意味に合うように，英文を完成させましょう。

(1) 隣の席が空いていても，そこに持ち物を置かないでください。

_____, please do not put your belongings there.

(2) 彼女は弁護士になるため，法学部に入学しました。(節になるように)

She entered the faculty of law _____.

(3) あなたは大学を卒業してしまったので，早く職を見つけるべきです。

_____ from college, you should find a job quickly.

3 指示がある場合はそれにしたがい，次の日本語を英語に直しましょう。

(1) あなたが幸せでありさえすれば，私はあなたのことは心配していません。

_____

(2) その大雨のため，私たちはグラウンドで野球の練習ができませんでした。

（「その大雨」を主語に）

_____

86

4 次の4つの項目を入れて，海外の食文化についての英文を作ってみましょう。

① 私たちが「ブルガリア」と聞いて真っ先に思い浮かぶのは「ヨーグルト」であろう。ブルガリアでは牛乳だけでなく羊の乳(sheep's milk)からもヨーグルトが作られる。

② ブルガリア人(Bulgarians)はヨーグルトをそのまま食べる(eat as it is)だけでなく，ヨーグルトでドレッシングやスープを作る。

③ また，ブルガリアではチーズの種類が豊富で，ブルガリアの人たちはほぼ毎日チーズを食べる。

④ ブルガリア人は長寿(live long lives)の人が多いので(given that ～)，私たちも試しにヨーグルトやチーズを食べる量を少し増やしてみるのもいいかもしれない(maybe we should)。

_____

_____

_____

_____

🔊 LISTENING

会話を聞いて，(1)～(4)の内容を書きとりましょう。

拓とエイミーが，友だちのハサンについて話しています。(*T*: Taku *A*: Amy)

T: Amy, listen! I cooked pork curry for Hasan, but he didn't eat it at all!

A: No, Taku. (1)_____, he would not eat the food because of his beliefs.

T: His beliefs? What do you mean?

A: In some countries, (2)_____. Have you ever heard about "halal food"?

T: Oh, I remember studying it in the home economics class. (3)_____.

A: We should keep learning about different cultures (4)_____.

(1) _____

(2) _____

(3) _____

(4) _____

2年の総合問題

教科書 pp.6-41

第1回　LESSON1 ～ 5

1 (　　)内から適切な語句を選びましょう。

(1) He (belongs / is belonging) to the music club.

(2) A TV (is / was) very expensive at that time.

(3) I (have worked / will be working) as a teacher by this time next year.

(4) The service (expects / is expected) to be available soon.

(5) He (must / can) have had a good rest because he looks relaxed.

(6) You (might well as / might as well) forget the terrible accident.

(7) How long (were you looking / had you been looking) for the key before you found it?

(8) The interview test will be (taken place / held) tomorrow.

(9) We (left / were left) the office door unlocked all night.

(10) How will the loss (make up for / be made up for)?

2 例にならって下線部の誤りを訂正し，文全体を書き直しましょう。

(例) My father always <u>keep my</u> promise. → My father always keeps his promise.

(1) We <u>had</u> dinner when the phone rang.

_____

(2) The league season <u>is beginning</u> in April every year.

_____

(3) You <u>had not better</u> underestimate her abilities.

_____

(4) We cannot emphasize the importance of understanding each other <u>very</u> much.

_____

(5) I was happy to see him yesterday because I <u>haven't</u> seen him in a long time.

_____

(6) I <u>didn't complete</u> the report yet, though I have to submit it tomorrow morning.

_____

(7) The driver's carelessness was <u>thought</u> the cause of the accident.

_____

(8) I was told <u>stop</u> by my grandparents' house.

_____

88

3 （　）内に与えられた語句を必要なら形を変えて使い，英文を完成させましょう。

(1) 彼はいつも食べ物のことばかり考えています。(think of)

_____

(2) 私は買い物に行くよりむしろ家にいたい。(would)

_____

(3) 生徒たちは今にも眠り込みそうに見えました。(fall asleep)

_____

4 （　）内の指示にしたがって，日本語の意味に合うように，英文を完成させましょう。

(1) 私たちは，彼はここに6時に到着すると聞きました。(過去進行形を使って)
　　We heard that _____ o'clock.

(2) そのピッチャーは次の試合に勝てば，10勝したことになります。
　　（「10勝する」= win ten games を形を変えて使って）
　　The pitcher _____ if he wins the next game.

(3) ここでしばらくお待ちいただけますか。(would を使って)
　　_____ a little while, please?

5 次の英文を日本語に訳しましょう。

(1) You should have moved the plan forward more carefully.

_____

(2) She is known as an expert in public health.

_____

2年の総合問題

教科書 pp.44-79

第2回　LESSON6 〜 10

1 日本語に合う英文になるように，空所に適切な語を入れましょう。

(1) 昨日よりずっと気分が良いです。

I'm feeling ＿＿＿＿＿＿ ＿＿＿＿＿＿ ＿＿＿＿＿＿ yesterday.

(2) トムは食費に月10万円もかかります。

Tom pays ＿＿＿＿＿＿ ＿＿＿＿＿＿ ＿＿＿＿＿＿ 100,000 yen a month for food.

(3) 宿題を終えた後に部屋を掃除しよう。

I will clean my room ＿＿＿＿＿＿ ＿＿＿＿＿＿ my ＿＿＿＿＿＿.

(4) 何か読み物はありますか。

Do you have ＿＿＿＿＿＿ ＿＿＿＿＿＿ ＿＿＿＿＿＿?

(5) 彼は友人たちから賞賛されてうれしかった。

He was ＿＿＿＿＿＿ ＿＿＿＿＿＿ ＿＿＿＿＿＿ praised by his friends.

(6) 子どもが私の周りを走り回って，仕事に集中できません。

I can't concentrate on my work ＿＿＿＿＿＿ my child ＿＿＿＿＿＿ around me.

2 日本語の意味に合うように，（　　）内の語句を並べかえましょう。

(1) その映画の後半は前半より面白くなかった。

The second half of the movie (the first / less / than / was / half / interesting).

＿＿＿＿＿＿＿＿＿＿＿＿＿＿＿＿＿＿＿＿＿＿＿＿＿＿＿＿＿＿＿＿＿＿

(2) できるだけ多くの問題に答えてください。

Answer (many / as / can / you / as / questions).

＿＿＿＿＿＿＿＿＿＿＿＿＿＿＿＿＿＿＿＿＿＿＿＿＿＿＿＿＿＿＿＿＿＿

(3) 私の両親は私が夜に外出するのを好みません。

My parents (going / me / don't / out / like) at night.

＿＿＿＿＿＿＿＿＿＿＿＿＿＿＿＿＿＿＿＿＿＿＿＿＿＿＿＿＿＿＿＿＿＿

(4) 私はそれを実行に移すのは難しいと思いました。

I (put / found / difficult / it / to) it into practice.

＿＿＿＿＿＿＿＿＿＿＿＿＿＿＿＿＿＿＿＿＿＿＿＿＿＿＿＿＿＿＿＿＿＿

(5) 私は母に子どもの面倒を見てもらいました。

I (my mother / of / take / care / had) my child.

＿＿＿＿＿＿＿＿＿＿＿＿＿＿＿＿＿＿＿＿＿＿＿＿＿＿＿＿＿＿＿＿＿＿

(6) 彼は自分の仕事が完成するのを見ることなく亡くなりました。

He did (completed / not / see / to / his work / live).

＿＿＿＿＿＿＿＿＿＿＿＿＿＿＿＿＿＿＿＿＿＿＿＿＿＿＿＿＿＿＿＿＿＿

90

3 ( )内に与えられた語句を必要なら形を変えて使い，指示がある場合はそれにしたがって，英文を完成させましょう。

(1) この市の人口は私の市の人口の 1.5 倍です。(large)

_____

(2) まもなく雨は止むでしょう。(stop ～ing)

_____

(3) 空から見ると，その町は美しいです。(分詞構文を使って)

_____

4 日本語の意味に合うように，英文を完成させましょう。

(1) コンテストの参加者は 4 名のみでした。

There were no _____ in the contest.

(2) 若い世代の人々は過去のことに責任がなくとも，未来のことには責任があります。

Even if _____ the past,

they are responsible for the future.

(3) 彼女のスピーチは聞く価値があります。

Her speech _____.

5 次の英文を日本語に訳しましょう。

(1) I want to make the most of this opportunity.

_____

(2) All things considered, it's a good deal.

_____

91

2年の総合問題
第3回 LESSON11〜14

教科書 pp.80-105

1 日本語に合う英文になるように，空所に適切な語を入れましょう。

(1) 最も子どもたちの関心を引くことをテーマに取り上げました。

I took up ＿＿＿＿＿ ＿＿＿＿＿ the children most as a theme.

(2) 壁が青く塗られている家が青木さんの家です。

The house ＿＿＿＿＿ ＿＿＿＿＿ are painted blue is Ms. Aoki's.

(3) 私たちの先生は私たちが困っている時はいつも助言してくれます。

Our teacher gives us advice ＿＿＿＿＿ ＿＿＿＿＿ ＿＿＿＿＿ in trouble.

(4) 彼はどんなに忙しくても，毎日，娘に絵本を読んであげます。

He reads picture books to his daughter every day ＿＿＿＿＿ ＿＿＿＿＿ he is.

(5) そういう訳で私は落ち込んでいるのです。

＿＿＿＿＿ ＿＿＿＿＿ I'm feeling down.

(6) 雨が降っていなかったら，ハイキングに行くことができるのに。

If it ＿＿＿＿＿ ＿＿＿＿＿ raining, I could go on a hike.

2 日本語の意味に合うように，（　　）内の語句を並べかえましょう。

(1) ここが私が借りるつもりのアパートの部屋です。

Here is (will / the apartment / that / rent / I).

＿＿＿＿＿＿＿＿＿＿＿＿＿＿＿＿＿＿＿＿＿＿＿＿＿

(2) この辺りに車を駐車する場所はありますか。

Are there any places around here (can / a car / where / park / we)?

＿＿＿＿＿＿＿＿＿＿＿＿＿＿＿＿＿＿＿＿＿＿＿＿＿

(3) 走っていたら，その列車に乗り遅れなかったかもしれません。

If I had run, I (missed / not / might / the train / have).

＿＿＿＿＿＿＿＿＿＿＿＿＿＿＿＿＿＿＿＿＿＿＿＿＿

(4) もし音楽がなければ，私はどのように暮らすのだろうか。

(for / it / not / if / were) music, how would I live my life?

＿＿＿＿＿＿＿＿＿＿＿＿＿＿＿＿＿＿＿＿＿＿＿＿＿

(5) この状況が続く限り，私たちは油断できません。

(this / as / persists / long / condition / as), we should be careful.

＿＿＿＿＿＿＿＿＿＿＿＿＿＿＿＿＿＿＿＿＿＿＿＿＿

(6) その男性スタッフはとても礼儀正しかったので，私はクレームを言いたくありませんでした。

The staff member (a man / so / that / polite / was) I didn't feel like complaining.

＿＿＿＿＿＿＿＿＿＿＿＿＿＿＿＿＿＿＿＿＿＿＿＿＿

3 ( )内に与えられた語句を必要なら形を変えて使い，指示がある場合はそれにしたがって，英文を完成させましょう。

(1) その小冊子は興味のある人ならだれにでもあげてください。

(booklet，複合関係代名詞を使って)

_____

(2) 彼は私たちにまるで私たちの先生であるかのように話します。(as if)

_____

(3) あなたはなぜここに来たのですか。(bring)

_____

4 指示がある場合はそれにしたがって，日本語の意味に合うように，英文を完成させましょう。

(1) その映画は始めはつまらないかもしれませんが，すぐに面白くなりますよ。

(関係代名詞を使って)

The movie, _____, will soon become interesting.

(2) 昨日小包が家に届いたが，その時私は家にいませんでした。(関係詞を使って)

A package arrived at my house yesterday, _____.

(3) あなたはこのボタンを押すだけでいいのです。

All _____ press this button.

5 次の英文を日本語に訳しましょう。

(1) I wish I had not asked him such a stupid question.

_____

(2) The sudden change in his schedule prevented him from attending the party.

_____

不規則動詞変化表

原形	現在形	過去形	過去分詞形	〜ing 形
be	am / is / are	was / were	been	being
bear	bear(s)	bore	born[borne]	bearing
become	become(s)	became	become	becoming
begin	begin(s)	began	begun	beginning
break	break(s)	broke	broken	breaking
bring	bring(s)	brought	brought	bringing
build	build(s)	built	built	building
burn	burn(s)	burned[burnt]	burned[burnt]	burning
buy	buy(s)	bought	bought	buying
catch	catch(es)	caught	caught	catching
choose	choose(s)	chose	chosen	choosing
come	come(s)	came	come	coming
cost	cost(s)	cost	cost	costing
creep	creep(s)	crept	crept	creeping
cut	cut(s)	cut	cut	cutting
deal	deal(s)	dealt	dealt	dealing
do	do(es)	did	done	doing
draw	draw(s)	drew	drawn	drawing
dream	dream(s)	dreamed[dreamt]	dreamed[dreamt]	dreaming
drink	drink(s)	drank	drunk	drinking
drive	drive(s)	drove	driven	driving
eat	eat(s)	ate	eaten	eating
feel	feel(s)	felt	felt	feeling
fight	fight(s)	fought	fought	fighting
find	find(s)	found	found	finding
fit	fit(s)	fit[fitted]	fit[fitted]	fitting
fly	fly / flies	flew	flown	flying
forget	forget(s)	forgot	forgot[forgotten]	forgetting
forgive	forgive(s)	forgave	forgiven	forgiving
get	get(s)	got	got[gotten]	getting
give	give(s)	gave	given	giving
go	go(es)	went	gone	going
grind	grind(s)	ground	ground	grinding
grow	grow(s)	grew	grown	growing
hang	hang(s)	hung[hanged]	hung[hanged]	hanging
have	have / has	had	had	having
hear	hear(s)	heard	heard	hearing
hide	hide(s)	hid	hidden[hid]	hiding
hit	hit(s)	hit	hit	hitting
hold	hold(s)	held	held	holding
hurt	hurt(s)	hurt	hurt	hurting
keep	keep(s)	kept	kept	keeping
know	know(s)	knew	known	knowing

原形	現在形	過去形	過去分詞形	〜ing 形
lead	lead(s)	led	led	leading
learn	learn(s)	learned[learnt]	learned[learnt]	learning
leave	leave(s)	left	left	leaving
lend	lend(s)	lent	lent	lending
let	let(s)	let	let	letting
lie (横になる)	lie(s)	lay	lain	lying
light	light(s)	lighted[lit]	lighted[lit]	lighting
lose	lose(s)	lost	lost	losing
make	make(s)	made	made	making
mean	mean(s)	meant	meant	meaning
meet	meet(s)	met	met	meeting
melt	melt(s)	melted	melted	melting
mistake	mistake(s)	mistook	mistaken	mistaking
overcome	overcome(s)	overcame	overcome	overcoming
put	put(s)	put	put	putting
read	read(s)	read	read	reading
ride	ride(s)	rode	ridden	riding
ring	ring(s)	rang	rung	ringing
rise	rise(s)	rose	risen	rising
run	run(s)	ran	run	running
say	say(s)	said	said	saying
see	see(s)	saw	seen	seeing
sell	sell(s)	sold	sold	selling
send	send(s)	sent	sent	sending
set	set(s)	set	set	setting
shake	shake(s)	shook	shaken	shaking
shoot	shoot(s)	shot	shot	shooting
show	show(s)	showed	shown[showed]	showing
sing	sing(s)	sang	sung	singing
sink	sink(s)	sank[sunk]	sunk[sunken]	sinking
sit	sit(s)	sat	sat	sitting
sleep	sleep(s)	slept	slept	sleeping
speak	speak(s)	spoke	spoken	speaking
spend	spend(s)	spent	spent	spending
spit	spit(s)	spit[spat]	spit[spat]	spitting
stand	stand(s)	stood	stood	standing
swim	swim(s)	swam	swum	swimming
take	take(s)	took	taken	taking
teach	teach(es)	taught	taught	teaching
tell	tell(s)	told	told	telling
think	think(s)	thought	thought	thinking
throw	throw(s)	threw	thrown	throwing
understand	understand(s)	understood	understood	understanding
wake	wake(s)	woke[waked]	woken[waked, woke]	waking
wear	wear(s)	wore	worn	wearing
win	win(s)	won	won	winning
write	write(s)	wrote	written	writing

形容詞・副詞比較変化表

❶ -er / -est をつける語

原級	比較級	最上級	意味
big	bigger	biggest	大きい
bright	brighter	brightest	明るい
busy	busier	busiest	忙しい
clean	cleaner	cleanest	きれいな
cold	colder	coldest	寒い
cool	cooler	coolest	かっこいい
cute	cuter	cutest	かわいい
early	earlier	earliest	早い, 早く
easy	easier	easiest	やさしい
fast	faster	fastest	速い, 速く
great	greater	greatest	すばらしい
happy	happier	happiest	幸福な
hard	harder	hardest	一生懸命に
heavy	heavier	heaviest	重い
high	higher	highest	高い, 高く
hot	hotter	hottest	熱い, 暑い

原級	比較級	最上級	意味
kind	kinder	kindest	親切な
large	larger	largest	大きい
late	later	latest	遅れた
light	lighter	lightest	明るい
long	longer	longest	長い
loud	louder	loudest	(音・声が)大きな
new	newer	newest	新しい
nice	nicer	nicest	よい
old	older	oldest	古い
safe	safer	safest	安全な
short	shorter	shortest	短い
small	smaller	smallest	小さい
soon	sooner	soonest	すぐに
strong	stronger	strongest	強い
tall	taller	tallest	背の高い
warm	warmer	warmest	暖かい, 温かい

❷ more / most をつける語

原級	比較級	最上級	意味
beautiful	more beautiful	most beautiful	美しい
careful	more careful	most careful	注意深い
dangerous	more dangerous	most dangerous	危険な
difficult	more difficult	most difficult	難しい
easily	more easily	most easily	たやすく
exciting	more exciting	most exciting	わくわくさせるような
expensive	more expensive	most expensive	高価な
famous	more famous	most famous	有名な
helpful	more helpful	most helpful	役に立つ
important	more important	most important	重要な
interesting	more interesting	most interesting	興味深い
popular	more popular	most popular	人気のある
useful	more useful	most useful	役に立つ
wonderful	more wonderful	most wonderful	すばらしい

❸ 不規則変化をする語

原級	比較級	最上級	意味
bad	worse	worst	悪い
good	better	best	よい
well	better	best	上手に

原級	比較級	最上級	意味
little	less	least	少ない, 小さい
many	more	most	(数が)たくさんの
much	more	most	(量が)たくさんの